The Internet for 50+

THE
Internet
FOR

50+

The Complete Guide
for Every Canadian Over 50

Andrew Dagys

PRENTICE HALL CANADA

Canadian Cataloguing in Publication Data

Dagys, Andrew
    The Internet for 50+: the complete guide for every Canadian over fifty

Includes index.
ISBN 0-13-776402-2

1. Internet (Computer network). 2. Middle aged persons -
Computer network resources. 3. Aged - Computer network
resources. I. Title.

ZA4201.D34 1997   025.06305244   C97-931684-7

© 1997 Andrew Dagys

Prentice Hall Canada Inc.
Scarborough, Ontario
A Division of Simon & Schuster/A Viacom Company

Prentice-Hall, Inc., Upper Saddle River, New Jersey
Prentice-Hall International (UK) Limited, London
Prentice-Hall of Australia, Pty. Limited, Sydney
Prentice-Hall Hispanoamericana, S.A., Mexico City
Prentice-Hall of India Private Limited, New Delhi
Prentice-Hall of Japan, Inc., Tokyo
Simon & Schuster Southeast Asia Private Limited, Singapore
Editora Prentice-Hall do Brasil, Ltda., Rio de Janeiro

ISBN 0-13-776402-2

Managing Editor: Robert Harris
Acquisitions Editor: Jill Lambert
Editor: Catharine Haggert
Editorial Assistant: Joan Whitman
Production Coordinator: Julie Preston
Art Direction: Mary Opper
Cover and Interior Design: Kevin Connolly Design
Cover Illustration: Greg Stevenson
Page Layout: Gail Ferreira Ng-A-Kien

1 2 3 4 5   W   01 00 99 98 97

Printed and bound in Canada

Visit the Prentice Hall Canada Web site! Send us your comments, browse our cata-
logues, and more. **www.phcanada.com**

To my wife, Dawn-Ava
and our children, Brendan and Megan

Contents

Foreword

Quite by accident, the Internet has provided unparalleled opportunities for mature Canadians to improve their quality of life. As an innovative tool for communication, discussion, and exchange of information, the Internet has become especially suited to meeting, in the most unique way, the special needs of retirees or near-retirees—Canadians over fifty.

The Internet is many things to many people, not the least of whom are retirees and near-retirees. The Internet combines the immediacy of television, radio, and telephone with the depth found in newspapers, books, and magazines. It does not "replace" anything. Rather, it is its own medium. A tool. A different way of achieving similar objectives. It can meet many of your needs.

The needs of retirees and near-retirees can traditionally be discussed in terms of personal finances and quality of life. Quality of life includes health considerations, housing options, and the use of one's leisure time. The Internet, in its own way, helps to meet most, if not all, of these needs!

A key objective of *The Internet For 50+* is to help you learn how to use the Internet. Another is to demonstrate why you would want to use it. In some cases, the Internet is the only way to meet your financial and quality-of-life needs. Therefore, this book will take you into the world of the Internet, break it down into its components, and introduce to you those online resources best suited to your needs and interests. This book will also steer you away from some of its aspects that can be considered to be a waste of time—and there are many such aspects!

Once you fully experience the Internet, its original mystique should be reduced to a simple realization that it is essentially a tool for communication, entertainment, learning, and exchange of information and creative ideas, with one big difference—all this is done in the comfort of your home!

If you are already on the Internet, or once you have learned how to use it, *The Internet for 50+* will help you address many of your retirement or near-retirement concerns. How? You will be provided with useful advice—finance and quality-of-life-related. Then, after key issues are introduced and discussed, you will be shown how to best use specific Internet resources as a tool to meet your special needs and information requirements. This novel approach (first introduced by Jim Carroll and Rick Broadhead, authors of several Internet books published by Prentice Hall) represents a significant and refreshing departure from what you have probably already seen by way of simple Internet "directories."

Recognizing that nothing can or should replace personal contact, the Internet is nonetheless a very useful and powerful supplementary tool of interaction, communication, and information gathering. It can be harnessed to overcome some of the typical constraints experienced by mature Canadians. The greatest of these constraints usually involve reduced mobility and a limited or fixed-income. It takes only one of these impediments to keep you from enjoying a better lifestyle, whether it limits your entertainment, education, or contact with others. But with the Internet, you can overcome these obstacles and still enjoy what life has to offer.

If you already own a computer, the extra cost of getting connected to the Internet is more than likely worth it, as this book will demonstrate. If you don't have a computer and are thinking of getting one, you've probably already observed that personal computer (PC) prices are dropping every month. However, one of the most critical developments with regards to affordable access to the Internet is the "network computer" (NC). A network computer is dedicated to accessing the Internet and other networks and doesn't include all of the extras typically found in a computer that is used for business and other purposes. This new technology is expected to cost under a thousand dollars and will facilitate economical access to the Internet. The increasing affordability of PCs, and the recent availability of NCs, places the Internet well within your grasp. These are crucial developments, especially for those on fixed incomes and for those who can not or are not inclined to invest thousands of dollars into a new emerging technology.

Acknowledgements

Writing a book is very much a collaborative effort and represents one of the true pinnacles of teamwork. As with any team, the individuals within it play different, but important roles. *The Internet For 50+* would not have been created were it not for the help of certain visionaries, contributors, and coordinators.

The Visionaries

Special thanks to Robert Harris and Jill Lambert of Prentice Hall Canada, who recognized the value of the Internet as a tool to meet the needs of men and women over fifty. They worked hard to shepherd, champion, and support this project to its fruition. I also thank David Tafler, of *CARP News*, who realized that the time had come for a book like *The Internet for 50+*, and who also threw his support behind the enterprise. To all of these hard-working professionals and visionaries, I give my thanks.

The Contributors

Many thanks to Catharine Haggert, my editor. It is she who usually injected the "art" into the "literature." It was a most pleasant experience to have worked with her—a very talented editor.

Some of the most valuable advice to be found in this book comes from the contributors of personal accounts—these are the true Internet pioneers! I thank these "co-writers" (and the many others who offered to share their experiences with the Internet but who were omitted only because of limited space). All are class acts!

Thanks to Harry Gilman and Michele Fleet—my technical-issue gurus!

My loving thanks to my wife, Dawn-Ava, who was a contributor by her support and never-ending patience.

The Coordinators and Producers

Many individuals at Prentice Hall Canada helped to create this book. But I owe special thanks to Karen Alliston, who was always available to skillfully answer my questions and to field my requests for endless courier deliveries. She was also instrumental in keeping the project on track, and her optimistic and light-hearted personality made the whole book-writing experience more than pleasurable!

Additional thanks to Judy Bunting, Sharon Sawyer, Steve Lewis, and all the others who worked behind-the-scenes at Prentice Hall Canada towards the successful completion of this book.

Another word of thanks to Jack David, publisher of my first book and profoundly-skilled writer. I know of few persons who can say so much in so few, well-chosen words. My gratitude for helping me to re-craft my career in a most unexpected yet fulfilling way!

Special Acknowledgment

When it comes to the relevance of the Internet for persons over fifty years of age, few individuals exude as much enthusiasm as Dan Goldhar, vice-president and general manager of Fifty-Plus.Net—the online voice of CARP. Dan is also a gifted TV and radio guest speaker. You will no doubt hear more from him in the near future. One of the key reasons that this book came to pass was Dan's commitment and belief in the importance of the Internet as a tool and resource for persons over fifty.

I'd like to especially thank Dan for supporting this book in so many ways. Through his experience and eagerness he contributed valuable and unique insights to this work, he secured many of the personal accounts to be found in the book, and he helped me in other ways when my schedule got tight.

A tireless, dedicated, and personable individual, Dan has been a pleasure to work with and more importantly, has been a friend throughout.

A Bird's Eye View

O ne thing is almost certain whether you're new to the Internet or not—you've been curious about its potential personal application to your needs, the needs of someone over fifty. *The Internet For 50+*, in addition to addressing and providing advice on many of these needs (Part II), endeavours to teach you *how* to use the Internet (Part I). In other words, the "nuts and bolts" of the Internet should be grasped before you can really appreciate the value of the Internet as a "tool." Difficult you say? Here's what Peter Weatherby (**pete_weatherby@prodigy.com**) had to say about his initial Internet experience.

Life before and after the Net

In 1994, a friend said that I should explore the Internet for ideas and information. I opened the "door" to the Internet and rather nervously looked in. At first it scared me. I felt like a tiny fish in a huge ocean. I had no idea where to go, what to look for. I was lost, swimming around in a vast, mind-boggling sea of data and subject matter.
But I soon learned that the Internet was like a library. First you need to know specifically what you are looking for. Then, you use a search engine to find it, and it takes

you to the "shelf" you want. The World Wide Web por-
tion of the Internet provided me with up-to-date infor-
mation on topics I enjoy—current events, countries,
cultures, postal news, travel, food, hobbies—everything
under the sun. I also use the Internet for e-mail "pen-
palling" and find it fascinating to receive messages in min-
utes from places as far apart as Uzbekistan, China,
Australia, and Russia.

For me, being a stay-at-home senior, using the Web has
been of enormous benefit. But for anyone 50+ (I am 70)
the Internet can be a window on the world, without leav-
ing one's living room.

This personal account is typical of the type of experience that new Internet users often share.

If you already know the technical in's and out's of the Internet, feel free to skip (or simply scan) Part I of this book. Or, if you wish, use it as a technical referral source from time to time.

With *The Internet For 50+*, you will also learn *why* Canadians over fifty use the Internet (Part II). In fact, most of this book is devoted to these "why's."

So, welcome to the world of the Internet! A little bit of time and practice spent on trial and error will almost certainly result in surprise after surprise as you learn more about this fascinating medium. And what the future holds is anyone's guess! Yet one thing is certain—this technology is here to stay. It may change and look different; but just as it's difficult to imagine society going back to horses and buggies, it's unlikely that people will reject the Internet. I think that once you start to explore it, neither will you.

How This Book Is Structured

When writing this book, I aimed to provide you, the reader, with maximum value. How did I do this?

The book has two main parts. The first, Part I, discusses the "how-to" issues of the Internet—the "nuts and bolts." The second, Part II, deals with *why* persons over fifty use the Internet. This book lays out all the issues for you in one stop.

In addition, throughout this book you will find practical, succinct advice on many "fifty-plus" issues such as finance, health, housing, and leisure. Personal accounts from existing Net users often echo this advice. Referrals to some of the most frequented sites on the Internet abound. Finally, an organized appendix of additional Internet sites (not discussed in the main body of this book) was researched and is included for your benefit.

The Internet has evolved considerably, even in just the last few years. It has evolved from a "browse me, I'll dazzle you" medium into a sophisticated, practical "what can I do for you?" medium. It was my intention for this book to match the current state of the Internet, with the specialized, value-added format that you will no doubt find throughout this book. It is time for Internet books to evolve away from the purely technical, cookie cutter type. Nowhere in this book will I write "Wow, look at this. Isn't this great!" Rather, key issues, general advice, and even personal accounts will be presented to you before Internet resources are first revealed. Then, you will be shown how to wield various Internet resources (tools) in your quest to fully address your "fifty-plus" needs.

A Ten-Minute Tour of the Internet

As for the Internet itself, what exactly is it? In a nutshell, the Internet is a network of linked computers, from the smallest personal computer (PC) to the largest mainframe. The resulting tangle of networks unites individuals, governments, businesses, schools, hospitals, and just about any other person or organization that uses a computer.

With the Internet, the key principle for users over fifty years of age to recognize is that if the Internet can do something for you that you previously used to do without it, then the Internet will likely do it better. Why? Because by nature the Internet is extremely efficient, progressively more economical, and very effective at meeting your needs and lifestyle goals in your retirement or near-retirement years. In addition, the Internet will allow you to do things that you may not have done before, like electronically viewing the text and pictures of Dead Sea Scrolls or scanning the background information and photos of the Smithsonian's many collections.

For the retiree or near-retiree, the Internet represents an array of tools and applications that can help meet personal needs and goals. The Internet may not only improve your financial and lifestyle goals—it may change the way you achieve them! For example, you can send PC-to-PC electronic mail to anyone, anywhere in the world. You can book your travel arrangements in the comfort of your home, after you have heard the sounds, seen the sights, and read the facts about your possible destination through the Web. You can even "chat" online to someone who's been there! The Internet may not only change how you do things, it may change what you do!

There are three components of the Net that you need to know about. In fact, these are the three "pillars" of the Internet. These components allow for communication, information gathering, and discussion. The three components of most relevance to persons over fifty and topics of discussion throughout this book, are:

- Electronic mail (e-mail)
- The World Wide Web (Web)
- Newsgroups and mailing lists (discussion groups)

One way of looking at these Internet tools or components is to consider them in the following light. You use e-mail to reach people and communicate with them; use the Web to find information; and use newsgroups and mailing lists to find people with specific information and to communicate with them.

E-mail

Specifically, e-mail is a way to type a message and send it to someone on the Internet. One of the first and most-used applications of the Internet, e-mail is a no frills way for people to communicate with each other—PC to PC. It's like leaving a message on an answering machine, except that you type it in. You have access to anyone in the world, and can communicate with them individually or send the same message to many people at one time You can engage in ongoing discussions, or ask for help, comments, or advice.

Think about the time you spend to get an envelope, write a letter by hand (correctly and on the first try), and then go to the post office to stamp it and mail it. While boomers and teens enjoy e-mail because of its timesaving or novelty attributes, for those over fifty, mobility (or lack thereof) may sometimes be the key issue. Internet e-mail is a great way to compensate for mobility-related problems.

E-mail software is getting easier to use all the time. In fact, because it's so easy, technical discussion in this book will be kept to basics. This is not to save paper! Rather, it's because I honestly believe that once the software is loaded into your computer, e-mail is really easy to use. With the built-in tutorial features of e-mail programs, the hands-on approach is actually the best way to learn.

The World Wide Web

By now, you have probably heard about the World Wide Web, better known as the "Web." This resource has intrigued and captured the imagination of the world. While e-mail is still the most oft-used Internet application for users over fifty, the Web is the fastest growing. Why? Because Web "pages" are creative, interactive, and appealing to the senses. This is so because the Web is an information-sharing tool that combines words, pictures, graphics, sound, and more and more often, video. All of these elements can be seen on your computer screen as if they were electronic pages. The pages reside on computers in different places, and each place is called a site.

You can access thousands of sites whose Web pages may be interlinked (hence the term "Web") to other sites anywhere in the World! How do you access these sites, filled with electronic pages? By using a browser—a search tool (software) designed to find and display Web pages scattered on the Internet.

The browser is very simple to use. However, what the browser actually does is far from simple. To illustrate, picture hundreds of books scattered on the floor of a gymnasium. You want to find information about automobiles. You know there must be an "automobile book" in the gymnasium, but you can't see it, and you also don't know its title or which other book(s) have chapters on "automobiles." That is what the Web is like. A browser, however, will not only find the "book(s)" (sites), it will also find you the "chapter(s)" (Web page(s)). A browser (such as Netscape Navigator or Microsoft Explorer) acts like a librarian. It is this perceived "network" that intimidates people and keeps them from using the Web. What they forget is that the software does the unpleasant, underlying "search" work for them; and the software itself is easy to use!

The Web offers a vast array of financial, health, housing, advocacy, and leisure-related resources. "Resources" is a catch-all term that is used precisely because the Web can give you so many different kinds of useful information! For example, you can listen to a talk show offered by the CBC a few hours ago and you can even download the text. You can watch a hurricane as it draws near to the coast of Madagascar. Or, you can watch in horror as your shares in an exploration company take a tumble in the last few hours of public trading!

Also, on the World Wide Web you can bank, shop, plan a trip to the store or across the world, research or discuss a particular health topic, or watch a video transmission. And there's more.

The World Wide Web is best experienced, not explained. To this end, discussion in Part I of this book is again restricted to the essential technical basics—enough detail to get you started, but not so much so as to lose sight of the ultimate objective of this book— to demonstrate why Canadians over fifty should (or do) use the Web and other tools of the Net.

Newsgroups and Mailing Lists

The Internet is home to a myriad of newsgroups. These are also referred to as discussion groups and reside on an electronic organizational "system" called USENET. Newsgroups resemble bulletin boards, and consist of a broad collection of daily postings, or "news", that deals with many, many different areas of interest. Topics range from the latest on healthy eating to the best way to handle leaky basements in your house! USENET newsgroups and electronic mailing lists are technically quite different from each other. Yet, both represent groups and forums of discussion.

Therefore, many of the reasons you would use newsgroups apply to the use of mailing lists. For example, both newsgroups and mailing lists represent a "special interest community" where persons with common interests exchange information and ideas. Mailing lists are similar to e-mail, but while e-mail is typically used for personal communication by "electronic letter," mailing lists are for both on-going, personal communication and on-going, multi-party discussion and information-sharing.

You are probably wondering what Internet newsgroups might hold for you. Well, I can guarantee you that you will find at least one newsgroup that is related to one topic of interest to you, be it bizarre or serious! Anyone can participate in newsgroups, whether you are asking for someone else's advice on a topic or offering some of your own. You can see everyone else's questions and other peoples' replies. Or, you can even post your own question to a newsgroup and look at one or a hundred replies! The key thing to recognize is that the playing field is wide open, and while most of the information is good-intentioned, some of it is junk.

Also, don't ignore the usefulness of mailing lists. A mailing list deposits all of the postings into your e-mail box, while you have to go and look at the postings to a newsgroup. You can post messages to a list, while receiving all messages posted to the list by others. Messages can be ignored, read, or replied to (to the sender or to the list). There are variations to the theme, which we will see later, but anyone with an e-mail address can subscribe to a mailing list. They are ideal for retirees or near-retirees since many focus strictly on "fifty-plus" issues such as personal finance, health, mobility, and leisure.

More detailed discussion of the "three pillars of the Internet" can be found in Part I—The New User's Guide to the Internet.

The Internet for 50+: The Benefits

As someone over fifty, you have specific issues to deal with—with or without the Internet. These key issues may be financial, health, housing, or leisure-related—and they won't go away. A cliché comes to mind: "You can do it the easy way, or you can do it the hard way." In most cases, the Internet represents the easier way. Your ability to draw on one resource or a combination of Web, e-mail, or newsgroup resources will help you deal with these key issues efficiently, economically, and effectively.

In addition, if you are currently working or are running your own business, you probably already use a personal computer. You've probably heard that taking it one step further (getting connected to the Net) will help your working life. An entire chapter is devoted to show you why those over fifty use the Net to help them with employment or business-related issues. In addition to maximizing your government entitlements and managing existing finances, your ability to actually generate additional income is one of the most important "fifty-plus" issues you will face.

If you are over fifty and are actually into retirement, the benefits of getting "wired" to the Internet are plenty. Even if you don't have a PC yet, the balance of the chapters in Part II of this book will, in my opinion, provide you with compelling reasons why getting a PC and getting connected to the Net makes sense. I'm convinced that the benefits will far outweigh the costs. Canada has some of the lowest-cost Internet access in the world, and the era of lower-cost PCs and NCs is nigh.

Using the Net yields many more personal benefits, such as education, entertainment, and the general broadening of your horizons. It's a different way of doing and looking at things. You can research and explore the universe of thoughts and ideas residing at your fingertips. You can share with your children and grandchildren the many new things you have seen on the Internet. You can also hear their stories—Internet-related or otherwise. We've all become accustomed to other technologies (VCR's, microwaves and cell phones are first to come to mind). Why not get accustomed to the Net?

Conclusion

The general benefits cited above are but the tip of the iceberg. In the end, the main benefit of using the Internet will likely be a very personal one. However, you now have an initial flavour as to why you may want to become a part of the Internet phenomenon.

The Internet also has an unpleasant side. The media, rightly so, quickly picks up on stories of Internet-related fraud and pornography. While it is true that the Net provides a conduit for fraud, pornography, and other vices, the Net is just that—a conduit. You don't have to receive these messages. You don't need to use this as an excuse to avoid the Internet any more than you would use the existence of phone-in, adult entertainment services to cut your phone service. Remember, you possess the control switch!

You should also expect technical problems to crop up as the Internet expands. Jammed phone lines, long downloading times, and other "surprises" may await you. But for every negative experience, there will usually be many, many more pleasant surprises for you—surprises that will more than likely help you improve your "fifty-plus" lifestyle!

PART I

The New User's Guide to the Internet

Chapter 1

The Nuts and Bolts of the Internet

What is the Internet? One way to answer this question is to picture all telephones as computers instead. That's the Internet! It's a lot of computers communicating with each other. Each computer collects information and makes some of it available to other computers. If you're Internet-connected, you have access to hundreds of thousands of other Internet-connected computers. Internet access means that you can call computers up and get information from them. Information can be in the form of text, sound, images, and graphics. A true step up from the telephone!

There are many ways to get connected; and there are many Internet "resources" that you can access (for example, persons with e-mail, World Wide Web pages, and topical newsgroups).

Getting Started

Know Your Personal Computer

If you've been using your PC for awhile, you'll probably have no trouble loading your Internet connection and browser software into it. But what if you're someone who wants to enter the world of the Internet all at once? You don't have a PC. You have no Internet account. What do you do? Who do you turn to? Fear not—the process is not as complicated as you may think!

If you haven't bought a computer yet, you may first want to buy a book or magazine on PCs. This will give you a better idea of what you can expect when you buy your first PC.

When you're ready to buy a PC, make sure you have at least 32 megabytes of random access memory (RAM—the space in which your applications run). Also make sure that you have enough storage capacity for these applications (3.2 "gigabytes" is more than enough room for today's complex software to reside in). The more RAM and the more gigabytes you have, the more you can do with your computer.

For many over fifty, eyesight may be an emerging issue. If this is the case with you, I recommend at least a 15-inch monitor; but getting a 17-inch one is probably worth the extra few hundred dollars. In other words, trade off other "extras" in favour of obtaining a better monitor if price is a key issue with you.

The key to entering the Internet is your modem, a device allowing for data transfer over a telephone line. Because the quality of your modem has a direct impact on the quality (speed) of Internet access, I strongly recommend at least 28.8 kbps (the rate at which data is transmitted from computer to computer). Faster modems (56 kbps) are available too, and some cable companies now offer super-fast cable connections.

One good source for information about setting up your computer is *The Computer Paper- Canada's Computer Information Source*. This tabloid is a free source of PC and Internet-related information. News, product reviews, and special features are provided each month. You can find free copies in most Canadian libraries and computer stores.

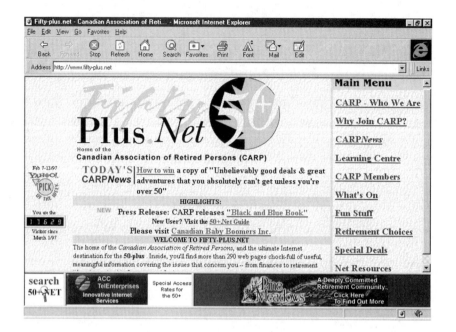

Fifty-Plus.Net (**http://www.fifty-plus.net**), the Canadian Association of Retired Person's (CARP) World Wide Web site, goes even further. It provides member discounts on a wide variety of products and services, including Internet access and computer hardware (equipment).

Internet Browsers

Much like different fax machines and telephones have various features and frills, the Internet allows for different types of software to access it. This means that the ease of searching the Internet, the variety of tools available in the software package, and the way that information looks on your screen all depend (to at least a certain extent) on your browser software selection.

The most popular browsers are Netscape Navigator and Microsoft's Internet Explorer. Most browsers combine e-mail, Web, and newsreader software into one software package to allow for "one-stop" access to the Internet.

The Web portion of the Internet is a worldwide network of computer servers. People, companies, and governments publish documents on their own servers; anyone on the Net can access, view, or download these documents or "pages" with their browser. The pages can contain any combination of text, pictures, audio, animation, or video—commonly referred to as "multimedia."

Getting Online

So you bought the software. What's your next step? Basically, you need to choose an Internet service provider (ISP) in order to get hooked up to the Internet. There are two basic types of ISPs:

- Commercial providers
- Full or partial service providers

When choosing between these services, you have to consider overall cost, services offered, and your Internet information needs. Because there are so many variations in services offered and so many ISPs, the best advice I can give you is to pick up a local Internet or computer magazine to see which ISP best meets your need at the lowest cost. In many cases, the magazine will rate the ISPs to help you with your decision.

Commercial Providers

You've probably heard of America Online (AOL), CompuServe and Prodigy. They all started out as closed networks (not Internet in the true sense) where you could only access their own computers. These services have since woken up to the intense interest in genuine Internet access—access to other people, organizations, and their varied resources.

Because they were selective in content from the start, and because they now provide a path to the Internet, you may want to consider commercial providers as a viable option. In many cases, they divide their resources into groups such as finance, health, housing, and lifestyle—issues that are especially interesting to those over fifty. The Microsoft Network (MSN) was the first to provide a hybrid of the commercial provider service (the commercial provider's proprietary content in addition to regular Internet access). Sympatico, a Canadian ISP, is continuously building more content to complement their original Internet access services. Both of these latter two service providers, like the original three, are large "hybrid commercial ISPs."

Full- or Partial-Service ISPs

Full-service ISPs provide one-stop Internet access. They give you all you need to get online—hookup software, a browser like Netscape Navigator, and other tools. Their services vary in that some give you choice of software while others require you to use only theirs. The setup process under full-service ISPs is as easy as the process for commercial ISPs. The difference is that with the former, you have a more flexible and often cheaper pricing structure.

Partial-service providers provide you with connectivity only. You may have to go out and buy your browser on your own. Since many PCs are sold Internet-ready (with browsers), this may not be a big issue. Still, the way by which you obtain the software you need to set up your account with the ISP is determined by the provider (that is, connection software can be sent to you by mail or can be downloaded from the provider's computer via your modem). Additional service and support may be good, average, or non-existent.

The advantage that partial-service providers have over all others is cost savings. Since it's cheaper, you may want to consider the full or partial ISP option, especially if a friend is able to help you out with Internet setup. Once you're connected, your Navigator or Explorer software is more than user-friendly enough to guide you from there. If you're already on the Net but you started out with a commercial provider, it may be time to consider a switch if cost is a growing concern.

What to Look for in an ISP

Not all ISPs are created equal, and you should therefore do some basic homework before signing on with one. Some points to consider include the following:

Cost Get all the facts about the fee structure offered by the ISP. Be on the lookout for hidden costs and compare the costs of at least two ISPs.

Access In addition to cost, one of your key objectives when dealing with ISPs is to ensure that they have a lot of phone lines. In other words, their lines should seldom be busy. To this effect, you ought to enquire if the ISP has a "no busy signal" policy or guarantee. In addition to asking the ISP for information on Internet accessibility, ask for a few references or talk to friends who already have a hookup with the ISP you are considering.

Speed Ask the ISP about the efficiency and speed of its link to the Internet. An efficient connection will result in faster downloads.

Support The ISP should be able to provide you with good support to any questions you may have or problems that you are experiencing. A professional and reliable "help desk" at your ISP is at least as important as the cost of the service provided. Ask the ISP about its support services.

Your Own Web Site You should also ask if the ISP will allow you to set up your own World Wide Web site if you choose to do so. While many ISPs offer a one- or two-page site for free, others will charge a fee.

Type of Internet Account

Once you have selected your provider, and having established a modem connection with the ISP, you must then give the ISP your user name and other information and request an "account". After obtaining this account (and a password), the ISP will provide you with one more thing—an Internet address. This address essentially attaches and places your PC unto the "highway" of the Internet. Now you are hooked-up!

Names and Numbers

Did you ever remember a telephone number by the letters on the keypad? Well the Internet is the same way. You could reach an Internet "address" by either using numbers or letters. Obviously, letters are easier to remember and are more personal, so they were adopted as "IP", or Internet Protocol. The IP address and the Domain Name System (discussed below) represent the "telephone directory listings" of Internet users. For a Web site address, they probably look something like the following:

http://www.fifty-plus.net
or
http://www.seniornet.org

These Web site "addresses" are also referred to as Uniform Resource Locators, or URLs (pronounced U-R-L, not "earl"). If you want to access a Web site you will need to find the URL.

Domain Names

If you use the services of an Internet Service Provider, you'll be assigned to the domain used by the ISP. The domain name identifies the computer that the ISP uses as a "base" for its customers. This domain name may end with ".net". Your e-mail address (provided to you when your account is opened) might look like **jdoe@abc.net,** where "abc.net" is the domain name of the ISP.

The letters after the last "dot" (period) depend on the type of domain that your ISP resides in. This last suffix of an Internet domain name is either a code for a country or a descriptive zone name. The two-character codes for countries are basically abbreviations, such as ".ca" for Canada. And if, say, a company is based in only one city, it may have a sub-domain name of "xyzco.toronto.on.ca". If the company is national in size, then "xyzco.ca" is typically used.

Zone names are descriptively assigned to companies (.com), non-profit and other organizations (.org), government (.gov), educational facilities (.edu), international bodies (.int), or ISPs and similar organizations (.net).

Stop, Look, and Listen

Before getting into a discussion about the three "pillars" of the Internet (e-mail, the Web, and newsgroups), it is necessary to pause to consider the suitability of computer technology to your current or potential physical circumstances. We saw previously that as someone over fifty, your eyesight may not be as sharp as it used to be. Monitor sizes and screen colours are very much an issue. And for anyone over seventy, hearing may no longer be acute. You've no doubt already heard that the Internet is about all about dazzling text, colours, animation, video, and stereo sound. Why bother with the Internet if you can't fully experience it?

The answer to these dilemmas is simple—you need not feel limited. This is because a handful of resourceful companies have developed "adaptive technologies." These advancements represent hardware and software modifications to help you use your computer more easily. For example, you can move your mouse pointer with voice recognition, arrow keys, an oversized track ball (like a mouse, but spherical), or with a special ergonomic keyboard. You can have your monitor screen magnified or have your text dictated by voice into a word processor. Even something as easy as purchasing a bigger PC monitor can make life easier for you.

Providers of Adaptive Technology

Co-Net represents the "yellow pages" of assistive technology, cataloguing just about every serious adaptive product available. You can search its database by keyword to find what you need. It has information on video magnification software, voice recognition systems, ergonomic peripherals, lap tables, and even special grab bars for better mobility.

For "senior" seniors, the reasons for using the Internet are as compelling as those for anyone else. I can't think of a better way to mitigate the isolating effects of impaired mobility or hearing than by using the Net! Adaptive technologies provide a bridge between physical limitations and access to the Internet.

As with anything that is not tailored to a very large market, it will cost a little more. But fortunately the costs are on their way down, and you won't need deep pockets anymore. Shop around. Co-Net (trademark name of Trace Research Center) is a logical starting point. You can access their Web site (perhaps initially with the help of others) at **http://www.trace.wisc.edu/tcel/**. (How to access Internet resources such as this Web site is discussed in chapter 2.)

From this point onward in this book, I have eliminated references to the *http://* part of the Web site URL. I did this to avoid excessive repetition. Your browser can be set to automatically include this URL prefix in its "address window." Or, you can click your mouse to place your cursor just after the *http://* and enter the new URL from there. Should a different protocol be referred to in this book, then its complete "address" will be provided. Quick reminders of this protocol will be dispersed throughout this book.

Similar adaptive technology Web sites worth a browse include:

- **www.dragonsys.com**   (voice recognition/dictation specialists)
- **www.optelec.com**   (magnification system specialists)
- **www.microsys.com**   (vision, hearing, and mobility enhancement)

Again, don't forget to enter http:// before the "www."

Chapter 2

The Three Pillars of the Internet

The Internet has gained rapid acceptance throughout North America (75% of Internet users reside there) and many parts the world. On business cards, television, and newspaper advertisements, for example, you are likely to see e-mail and Web addresses. These addresses are easily recognizable. People want to reach others and also want to be reached themselves.

The three most significant components of the Internet are:

- E-mail
- The World Wide Web
- Newsgroups and Mailing Lists

E-mail: The Why's and How's

For Canadians over fifty, e-mail is the most popular Internet application. E-mail has the capacity to bring the world to your doorstep, or at least bring 50 million of its residents! (This is an estimate of how many individuals and organizations now use the Internet.) It's fast (instant transmission), efficient (no trips to the mailbox or post office), and economical (one e-mail message can be copied or duplicated to hundreds of other e-mail users).

When you obtain an Internet account, you also get a personal e-mail address. It enables anyone on the Net to send you a message. From this address, you can also send e-mail to others. An e-mail program (purchased separately or a part of your browser) allows for the transmission or receipt of e-mail messages over the Internet. The messages you receive initially pass through the computer (or server) of your ISP.

E-mail is now evolving beyond text-only applications. Messages will soon contain sound, images, video, digitized files, and other media. And now, e-mail is accessible through new "Personal Communications System" technology that is portable and wireless. It's growing in use by the day.

Why Mature Canadians Use E-mail

There are many reasons why you, a mature Canadian, may want to use e-mail. Several follow.

Easier Communication As mentioned earlier, one of the biggest impediments faced by retired persons may be the restriction of mobility. The process of mailing a letter, for example, involves manipulating an envelope and walking potentially long distances to the mailbox. E-mail does not require these things. And although many would say that e-mail is impersonal and lacks tradition, I would counter that its ease of use actually promotes communication. This brings me to my next point.

Promotes Face-To-Face Communication You likely place a premium on face-to-face, interpersonal contact. However, you have to keep in mind the following as you read through this section: e-mail is not intended to replace face-to-face interaction with people. What it does do, however, is create the opportunity to have more face-to-face contact by exposing you to more people! It's a catalyst for meeting people! So in addition to promoting more frequent communication with the same people, it promotes more communication with new people!

Promotes More Contact with Family There's a good chance that one or more of your kids have access to the Internet, be it at work or at home. This means that you can e-mail them at any time. Like a message left with an answering machine, they can open an e-mail message at any time. It's a great supplementary way to get a message across without feeling that you're imposing—something that you should never feel in the first place!

Promotes Other Types of Contact It's a fact that some people are reluctant to communicate one-on-one in certain situations, and actually would prefer the e-mail option. One person once told me that she used e-mail to let someone know that she was offended by a certain remark made in her presence. Preferring to avoid direct confrontation with her sometimes-abrasive acquaintance, she simply fired off the message. Unlike using a letter, when the moment may be lost or forgotten, she quickly sent a message and got back an equally-swift reply. It was an apology and a dinner invitation! This is a perfect example of one of the Internet's subtleties that are quickly being picked up and embraced by many e-mail users. These users see e-mail for what it is—a tool; but one that promotes positive communication.

Networking Is Easy E-mail helps you network with people. Sending a message to five, ten, or twenty people at the same time can trigger an avalanche of replies, visits, phone calls, or lunch invitations! In addition, any one of the recipients of your message could in turn forward it to others at a push of a button! Since as a retiree or near-retiree you may have more time to interact with others, the ability to meet new people, break new ground, and communicate with existing friends in this new way represents a significant contribution to a better retirement lifestyle.

It's Not Prohibitively Expensive While a PC or NC, and an ISP hookup costs money, you must recognize that a PC or NC can be used for many other things. As for e-mail (once you're online), it's generally cheaper than courier, fax, or even many long-distance telephone calls. If you run a home business, the savings can be significant. You can copy the same message to many other persons with one transmission. Economy of use is one of the key driving forces behind e-mail's current growth, acceptance, and success.

Its Easy to Use Even for Those without Computer Experience Another key driving force behind e-mail is ease of use. This is because most software packages that include e-mail are "windows friendly." In other words, the software facilitates the use of point-and-click technology. Screens are pre-formatted so all you have to do is type in your name, the destination, and the message.

True, e-mail (and the Internet) takes some learning. But I am convinced that for anyone over fifty, especially those persons with a little extra time on their hands, the initial investment in time would soon be outweighed by the benefits. As the Internet grows, as it becomes cheaper to use, and as it is embraced by even more persons over fifty years of age, its benefit and reach will be profound.

The Nuts and Bolts of E-mail

What E-mail Can Do

The best way to describe what good e-mail software can do is to first see what e-mail looks like. A message has three key parts: the heading, the text of the message and a digital signature. The following represents standard e-mail format:

Date Sent: Fri, 24 Oct 1997 10:22:56 -0200

To: jan_white@sympatico.ca

From: dsmith@herco.com

Subject: trip

Greetings from Albany! Just wondering if I can come up to Calgary next Tuesday and stay with you overnight. I'm on a business trip and all of the good hotels are booked.

Regards,

Dana Smith

Dana Smith, 123 East Street, Albany, New York 10056 782-7907

e-mail: dsmith@herco.com www:http://www.herco.com

The above-noted format is quite typical of most e-mail messages.

A big difference between Internet e-mail and printed memos (and letters) is that e-mail is more flexible. E-mail can be carbon copied (cc'd) to a very large number of other e-mail users. Most e-mail also has a "reply" feature where, at the push of a button, all you have to do to reply to a message is type in your response.

In addition to creating a message, you can receive messages too. Your e-mail software will create an "in box" for you where all in-coming messages are held until you open them. Even before open-ing these messages, you will have an idea as to what is in them since your "new mail" screen will probably have separate columns showing who the message is from, what the subject is, and the date and time the e-mail was sent.

You can delete, save, or print the message. However, one of the strongest features of e-mail is its ability to send or receive a computer file. This file can be a basic graphic, such as a greeting card, or can be a full report written in Microsoft Word, Corel WordPerfect, or just about any other word processing software package available.

The power of e-mail is what makes this the most-used tool of the Internet. (The Web, however, with all of its attendant bells and whistles, is the fastest growing.)

Electronic Postal Codes

Just like you would if you sent a letter to a friend, you'll need to know the recipient's address before you send your e-mail. A typical e-mail address contains a "name," followed by an "at" or "@" character preceding the domain name. This domain name is usually that of a host organization (business, ISP, government, or institution). Most host names (domain names) end in a three letter suffix (recall that ".com" signifies a commercial host).

The e-mail name before the @ symbol may look like "Ned.Gordon," "NGordon," "Ngordon," "Ned_Gordon," or other variations. Often you are asked what e-mail address you would like, other times the ISP assigns you an e-mail address. If you access the Internet through an ISP, your ISP's domain name usually appears after the @ symbol. For example, your address may look like "Your.name@isp.net."

If you get a returned e-mail message, check the spelling in the original e-mail address first. Addresses are meant to be precise and are prone to typos. But don't be surprised if the address no longer exists. Internet addresses change frequently, especially when the person you are trying to reach changes ISP.

Composing an E-mail Message

Because e-mail is broad in scope, fast in transmission, and easily saved, you need to be careful about what you send. People may not understand what you're saying which may result in misunderstanding. This is especially true when you're copying your message to someone. Think before pressing the send button and remember the "courtesy tips" listed below.

- Make your subject line as clear as possible. Too short is ineffective. Too long is unprofessional! Three to five words is best.
- Never answer a message in anger! Think clearly about your potential reply. Others may read this message if the person you send it to passes it on, so don't set yourself up for embarrassment!
- Recap the message to which you are replying; or use the reply feature of your software whenever you can. This will remind your recipient about what you are referring to.
- Be ***>>creative<<*** in your quest to be emphatic!!! Use your keypads with imagination. Most e-mail programs do not allow you to underline words, or to put them in bold or italic. But remember that overusing creative emphasis is irritating to the reader.
- Avoid "carbon copying" your message unless it is critical to do so. Ensure that all recipients will be interested in your message. An overfilled mailbox is an irritant to an Internet user!

How to Find Someone with the Net

If you're over fifty, you will have met a lot of people in your life. One way or another, you may want to contact some of them one day, especially after realizing how easy it is to do this using the Internet as a tool.

There are no complete "white or yellow pages" for the Internet as a whole. There are simply too many addresses for such an undertaking. Often, the most logical approach may be to start with a phone call to the person you are trying to contact. But what if you don't even know the telephone number?

Canada 411—The Phone Directory for Everyone—is an effective (fast) and economical (you don't have to buy a national CD ROM telephone directory) way to get a phone number. Its Web page (**www.canada411.sympatico.ca**) prompts you to enter the name and probable location of the person you're looking for. (It even searches for business numbers and locations.) If you know where they live, that's even better. It has over ten million listings of individuals and businesses and is useful for more than just finding e-mail addresses. It's also a great way to keep track of old friends. Similar resources include Four11 (**four11.com**), WhoWhere (**www.whowhere.com**), and ABII (**www.abii.com**). Alternately, you can use the smaller LookUp database at **www.lookup.com/lookup/search.html**. All of these resources can assist you if you think that the person you're looking for is online. We'll discuss how to access Web pages in the next section.

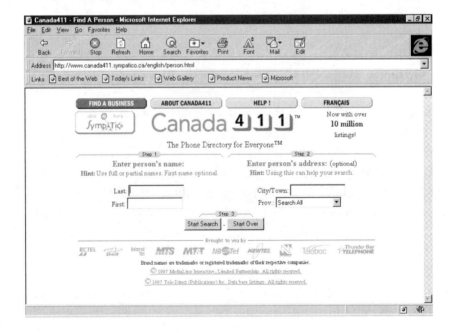

Pitfalls to Be Aware of

You should be aware of a few negative aspects of e-mail. There's no guarantee of fast message delivery. You can never be absolutely sure that your message got through, either. Likewise, you can't tell if your message was opened.

Internet e-mail is not secure. Although most messages are mostly harmless, you may want to think twice before discussing anything personal such as your financial or health status on the Internet!

The World Wide Web

The World Wide Web (commonly referred to as the Web), is all about information. So what's all the big fuss about it? I mean, in just about every newspaper, TV show, or radio broadcast you're just about bombarded with references to the Web! Let's see what the Web may have in store for you.

Would the Web Tangle You?

The Web's world popularity really stems from the fact that it can do everything a newspaper, TV, and radio can do at once—and more. A Web "site" (the host computer's location), like a combination of all these three media, allows for simultaneous text, sound, video, and graphics to appear on its "pages" (screen images stored in computer files). These often-simultaneous special effects are called "multimedia." Web pages are the sight and sound of the Net.

- Web-based multimedia is a very new and creative way of *presenting* information to you.

Web sites allow you to jump (or "link") to any other Web site in the world by clicking your mouse on specially marked words or pictures on the Web page. (If you're a "newbie," you should know that a mouse is a device that lets you move the cursor in a more flexible manner.) The items that you click are called "hyperlinks", and are written in what is called hypertext markup language (HTML). Web pages with these links have the potential to provide you with more information than either newspaper, TV, or radio can deliver; and it's all in one spot!

- The Web is far-reaching and *comprehensive*, thus providing good value for money.

With the Web, there is probably a "fifty-plus", issues-oriented site that deals with something that is of interest to you.

- The Web is a *relevant* tool.

If you follow the financial markets, you can see share prices updated in real time (as it happens). If you want to know about a retirement community in Australia, there's a Web page that can take you there. And if it's European soccer that you like, but you live in the United States, there is a Web page that keeps you posted on the scores in real time. You don't have to wait for newspaper delivery, the 6 o'clock TV news, or the 11 PM sports radio update.

- The Web is *fast* and can take you to information sources quickly.

Web sites are easy to access. Software allows you to travel from Web page to Web page at the click of a mouse. With Web browsing software, you don't have to learn any special computer language or follow detailed instructions.

- Browsing the Web is *easy* for anyone over fifty!

The Web lets you "move around." Given that many older Canadians have limited mobility (physiologically or in terms of transportation), the Web now allows them to participate in information gathering that was not possible to do before. A trip to the library in a snowstorm is not most people's idea of a pleasant experience.

- The Web keeps you *mobile*.

Mature Canadians typically like to know about the community events that go on in their neighbourhood. Although these events are often publicized by mail, newspaper, and radio, you may have missed printed community bulletins.

- The Web puts you "in the know" and is very *current*.

Millions of people, companies, and other organizations are on the Web. The Web changes minute-by-minute as more sites and Web pages pop up everywhere around the world. There is no roadway or "bulls-eye" to the Web; and a Web page in Canada can instantly link you to another in Europe.

- The Web is *fluid*, *growing*, and *dynamic*.

There is no complete directory to the Web, but there are tools (browsers) to make your search for information easier. What's more, anyone can build an index of their favourite Web sites.

- The Web can be untangled into something more *organized*— useful information.

Now you have a better picture of the Web: creatively presented, comprehensive, valuable, relevant, fast, easy to use, current, growing, and organisable—attributes that make it harder for you not to get tangled into the benefits of the Web!

With these benefits in mind, you're probably now wondering how much I've exaggerated them compared to the facts. Good question. Judging from several surveys, it is apparent that older Americans and Canadians alike have embraced the Internet.

Time Spent Several recent surveys have shown that retirees and near-retirees have taken the lead in terms of the time spent using their PCs. One survey (conducted by Packard Bell) revealed that while male adults between twenty and fifty spent nine hours per week on their PCs, those over fifty were found to spend 12 hours per week.

Size According to *CARP News*, CARP's monthly magazine, Statistics Canada reported that there are already over 200 000 Canadians over fifty on the Net. This number is growing steadily as the first of the baby boomers enter their fifties.

Growth An Intel survey found that the retired population was the fastest-growing segment of the PC-user market and therefore the overall Internet-user market.

Preference Most surveys of mature Internet users reveal that their key interest is writing correspondence (e-mail). Closely following e-mail as a popular application is researching financial issues and leisure options on the Web.

The Nuts and Bolts of the Web

Let's now turn our sights to the technical side of the Web. What type of software do you need? How does the Web actually work? How can you find Web information that interests you? These and other issues will be addressed next.

Web Browsers to Guide You

You'll need software (browsers) to get on the Web; and the browsers you need are getting more powerful and user-friendly all the time! Browsers (such as Netscape Navigator or Microsoft Internet Explorer) are powerful because most versions will allow you to receive all or most of the text, sound, graphic, or video information found on Web sites today. They are easy to use because Web sites can be accessed with only a few clicks of the mouse and a few strokes of the keyboard. Browsers do a good job of "guiding you" through the Web searching process.

Browsers take care of the "hard stuff:" they search the Web, extract and convert information back into your PC, and do other Internet-related tasks. They usually include e-mail and newsgroup newsreader applications. As for features and value-for-money, Netscape Navigator and Microsoft Explorer are very close in features throughout most of their browser lines. You can usually obtain and try out basic versions of both for free.

Web Addresses

Web browsers allow you to get connected with a Web server containing the Web page you are interested in. The server (and its pages) could be located anywhere in the world. Your browser uses the URL (Uniform Resource Locator) you type in to take you to a Web site. The URL is the address where the server that you want to access can be found. If you don't know the URL, you can also use your browser to access keyword search tools. More on this later.

As mentioned before, the information contained in a Web page is typically found in a format called HTML (hypertext markup language). HTML data is picked up by your browser, decoded, and presented to you in a readable format. The Web page may be on a computer server owned by a company, university, or the government, or it may be located on a server at an ISP or other location. The server will house an array of pages in HTML format. Each Web page has a unique identity—a home-page-related but distinct URL or "address." The URL is what you often see when a Web page is advertised, say, in a publication. For example, one of many URLs (pages) of Fifty Plus Net is:

http://www.fifty-plus.net/learn/main.html

The "http://" component represents the type of service you have accessed. This type means that the server is running hypertext transmission protocol that supports the linking of documents. Whenever you see this prefix, you pretty well know that it's a Web address. There are other types. These include Gopher servers (gopher://), FTP locations (ftp://), secure Web sites (https://), and Telnet locations (telnet://). But most of these are being superseded by the Web (because the Web can now access the same information that these latter types used to access).

Again, throughout this book you will be provided with the URLs of useful Web sites. I have omitted the prefix http:// in all cases except where another prefix, such as ftp://, applies. In these few cases, the full URL is provided.

Returning to the previous example, the component "www.fifty-plus.net", is the name and location of the server. This extension is mandatory information. The "learn/main.html" component of the URL is the page file name containing HTML-formatted page information. This last component describes the directory path to follow on the server to find a specific page and is not mandatory. If omitted, a "home page" will appear in most cases. Home pages will lead you to the content of all associated pages linked together in hypertext. It acts like a table of contents in a lot of ways, and often provides basic information about the entire Web site.

The Search Is On!

There are many ways to search for Web information. You can casually and randomly browse some Web pages and their "content" of topics. This is called "surfing."

You can also conduct very detailed research on a topic of interest to you. For subject- or name-driven searches of information where you don't know the URL, you can utilize a Web directory; or you can utilize a search engine (search tool). These and other ways of searching the Web by yourself are discussed next.

Surfing the Net

"Surfing the Net" is an expression that describes a nonchalant way of browsing Web, newsgroup, and other resources. "Surfing the Web" is probably a more accurate expression—this is where the sights and sounds are, and where most people actually spend their "Net" time.

When you surf, it's kind of like a Sunday drive! For example, you may be planning a trip and want to see a few pictures of Whistler British Columbia on a B.C. tourism agency Web site. Clicking once on your mouse may take you to a Web site showing average weather conditions in that area. Clicking another button, you may find yourself on a skiing-related discussion group. One last click and you're on a Web page describing the skiing industry! So you now see how easy it is to get distracted from your original goal—researching a trip to B.C.!

Locating Information with Directories

Directories are good first stops when starting subject or name searches. They are organized collections of topics and names that you can scan or search through. The biggest directory is called Yahoo. If you haven't heard of this name before, get used to it—you'll be hearing it throughout this book! Smaller directories also exist, usually geared to a smaller, more specialized audience (one example is a medical directory).

Yahoo's directory (**www.yahoo.com**) shown below, prompts you to key in a search phrase so as to provide you with a listing of all Internet locations with, say, the phrase "retirement." You may see a listing of twenty items. Clicking on the item titled "communities", you find a further list of retirement homes, and so on. Your final selection may take you (link you) right into a retirement home operator's Web page. Yahoo also has a convenient and recognizable set of links to search engines. Yahoo is thus a strong one-stop search destination. However, there is one drawback with Yahoo—your search results may number in the hundreds! What would you do then?

First, consider using the Canadian Yahoo (**www.yahoo.ca**) for Canadian results, as appropriate. Or, you may want to consider other directories such as those listed on page 28.

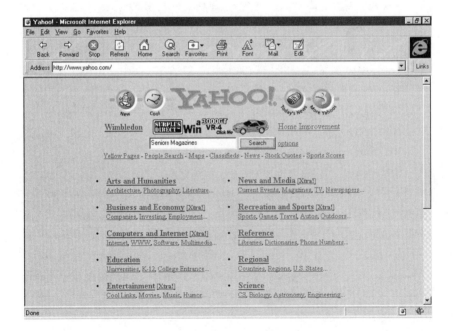

Selected Directories

Nynex's Big Yellow	**www.niyp.com**
Magellan	**magellan.mckinley.com**
Internet Sleuth	**www.isleuth.com**
New Rider's Yellow Pages	**www.mcp.com/nrp/wwwyp/**
Starting Point	**www.stpt.com**
Galaxy	**galaxy.einet.net**
Linkstar	**www.linkstar.com**
Clearinghouse	**www.clearinghouse.net**

Nynex's Big Yellow is a large business directory. It helps you to locate products or services geared to your special needs. However, it's mostly American in focus.

Magellan allows you to search "ranked" and "well-rated" Web sites. The rankings are made by individuals, and are not infallible. Yet, these directories provide you with a much more manageable list of results

Internet Sleuth has one of the most comprehensive collections of searchable databases around. It offers specialized searches by category. Like Yahoo, it can be a valuable referral resource for the special needs and interests of mature Canadians.

Galaxy provides references to articles, book excerpts, news, weather, a business directory, and more.

Don't forget: if you know the Web address already, you can go there directly (via URL). Also, many organizations print their Web "addresses" on their stationary or business cards. Hold on to the address of a site that you know you may want to browse or search later. It's a lot easier to jot down a Web address now than it is to conduct a time-consuming Web search later!

Locating Information with Search Engines

Search engines (also referred to as "search tools" or "Web robots") all do the same thing—they find information on the Web. Search engines, unlike most directories, depend on software (rather than people). Search engines automatically and periodically search for new resources from the Web by sending out "spiders," which are digital compilers of Web information. Thus, they re-generate their large indices of Web pages from time to time. When you request information (by starting a keyword search), you are asking the search tool to search the historical indices that have already been built. It's not usually a live search of the Web, contrary to popular belief.

Some of your choices of search engines may include the tools listed below.

Selected Search Engines

Alta Vista	**www.altavista.digital.com**
Excite	**www.excite.com**
Lycos	**www.lycos.com**
HotBot	**www.hotbot.com**
OpenText	**www.opentext.com**
InfoSeek	**www.infoseek.com**
WebCrawler	**www.webcrawler.com**

As you can see from the screen images of several actual Web directory home pages, the choices look similar—too similar. Therefore, let's run through some of the differences.

Alta Vista allows for searches by keywords or phrases. It's a large database and lists results in order of relevance.

Excite contains searches of a multitude of Web pages and recent Usenet news. It has links to current events, weather, sports and other issues. It presents results in summary, annotated form.

Lycos is best used to search a large database with keywords. It lists results in order of relevance. It also provides the first fifty words of each page that it retrieves for you.

HotBot is typically used to search the full text of a large database. It is one of the largest search engine databases on the Net. Results, however, are not always listed in order of relevance.

OpenText allows for a search of the full text of Web home pages by keyword or phrase. It is a relatively smaller database.

InfoSeek is a hybrid of OpenText and HotBot and is known for its relatively high speed.

WebCrawler returns a comprehensive list of Web links. It scans the full text of pages and is good at locating keywords embedded in them.

This, I believe, is all that you need to know for the time being.

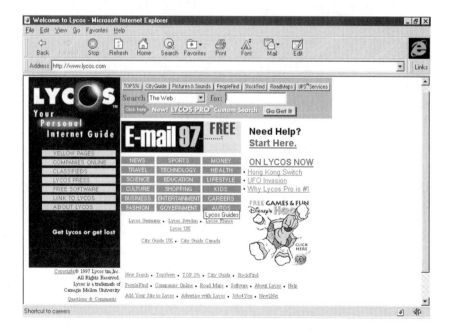

After you have done enough Web searching on your own and can no longer be considered a "new user," I believe that you'll see firsthand how easy it really is to use the Net!

Pitfalls You May Encounter

- When a new site comes out, many will try to get on it. A server can only take on so many "hits" or visits at one time. The result for you is a long wait. The best thing to do is to wait a few days and try again.
- Sites also become outdated. You will know that a link failed when you see an "Error 404" message.
- Transmitting and downloading special information such as graphics may take extra time. Be patient (or exit the site if the wait is unacceptable).
- The Web also contains a lot of garbage. It can be offensive and a waste of time.
- The Web is so big that it creates information overload. The best way to overcome this is to know what you really want from the Internet up front and stick to your search plan! For the retired person, the Web should be utilized more as a tool and less as a "time filler".

Usenet Newsgroups and Mailing Lists

We saw how valuable e-mail could be as a communication tool. We also saw how useful the Web could be as a way to get information in various forms. Although dazzling and extremely flexible in nature, the Web sometimes lacks the interactive touch. A more "personal" approach is often an effective alternative to accessing select information.

USENET newsgroups and mailing lists provide these more

interactive and personal approaches. These two topical resources are excellent Internet tools for retirees and near-retirees who, for example, want to:

- Find an answer to a common medical, legal, or other subject-oriented question
- Be up-to-date on special events or "fifty-plus" happenings.
- Receive online financial newsletters from individuals or organizations.
- Participate in casual discussions with a select group of other persons on a wide variety of other topics.
- Answer questions posted (posed) by other persons on topics which they are very knowledgeable in.

The above, and more, can be done through two components of the Internet—USENET newsgroups and mailing lists, each with its own characteristics. With them, you can passively track topical information, actively seek answers, or discuss issues of interest to you with others.

Newsgroups vs. Mailing Lists

The first resource, USENET, is an Internet system by which information is exchanged on countless topics. Each topic has its own discussion forum called a "newsgroup." There are currently about 25 000 newsgroups around the world and the number continues to grow. About 60% of these function in the English language. The second resource, mailing lists, represents organized lists of e-mail addresses. Each list is made up of people who have indicated an interest in a particular topic. People usually have to make a request (to the mailing list's own address) to be placed on such a list.

Often there are newsgroups and mailing lists on the same topic.

Both newsgroups and mailing lists allow you to be associated with a special group in order to get information or to discuss a topic with others in the group.

The most obvious difference between these two similar information sources is how you get the information. With newsgroups, you need newsreader software that allows you to read or post messages from/to USENET. By comparison, anyone with an e-mail address can join a mailing list. Information comes in with your regular e-mail. Most browsers (like Netscape Navigator or Microsoft's Explorer) accommodate both newsgroups and mailing lists.

Newsgroup information can be obtained by subscribing with the newsgroup of interest to you. Most Internet service providers offer this service. Conversely, you can get on a mailing list by sending a special e-mail message to the list management system or "listserver."

USENET allows you to subscribe to any newsgroup that your ISP provides, take in (read) any information sent to the newsgroup or give out (post) information to it. Each posting is called an "article" which can be commented on or replied to directly by e-mail.

Newsgroup postings are usually edited to some extent before release. Information is often well-organized and free. Newsgroup news articles are not received in e-mail boxes. Rather, they are transmitted to you in a batch upon your request, and interpreted and organized by newsreader software. Articles are meant for very broad distribution.

A newsgroup posting may invite one or a hundred responses! The responses may occur instantly or several weeks later!

Mailing list information can be put out by anyone with little interference and can involve a fee for things such as newsletters. Distribution is limited and targeted to specific users.

The discussion that follows will show you how you can use this special part of the Internet, how it works, how to find a topic or mailing list and other pointers. For the retired person with a bit of extra time on their hands, this can be one of the most rewarding and satisfying parts of the Internet. It combines the ability to communicate with others with information gathering on topics that are of personal interest.

USENET Newsgroups and Mature Canadians

If you are like most people, and you enjoy talking about something that interests you, newsgroups may be the place for you. As someone over fifty, you are likely looking at ways to enhance your lifestyle. This may involve a new hobby or a desire to re-educate yourself. Either way, you'll need information. USENET will likely have the information you are looking for. While a newsgroup (topic) may not be as structured as a college curriculum, it is nonetheless invaluable. As an information source, USENET is fast, economical, and includes the observations of more than one person.

With USENET, you can join newsgroups of interest to you. This book refers to many newsgroups dealing with topics that may be of particular interest to retirees and near-retirees. Knowing which newsgroups are out there on any one topic can save you considerable time searching for information.

One attribute of newsgroups that is very agreeable with retirees is that newsgroup culture is based on voluntarism. Simply stated, USENET is not there for the purpose of doing business. While there are some newsgroups that have a commercial component, sales are usually a by-product of a question such as "does anyone have a 1938 stamp of Australia?" However, anyone attempting some blatant advertising will likely be met with a barrage of nasty replies. This situation is referred to as "flaming."

No one owns or centrally administers USENET. Instead, it is put together with the collaboration of volunteers who compile information. As a result, newsgroups will continue to evolve to include more "fifty-plus" categories, where the majority of contributors are fellow retirees or near-retirees sharing common ideas and concerns.

The Nuts and Bolts of Newsgroups

Newsreader Software

To access a newsgroup, you will need newsreader software. With it, you can "subscribe" to newsgroups without much fanfare! Subscribing to a newsgroup involves telling your newsreader software that you want to see the postings from that newsgroup. Among the thousands of available newsgroups you can find a relevant newsgroup by keying in a "keyword," much like you would use a Web search engine. Once you subscribe to the newsgroup of your choice, you can post an article or "follow-up," a term used to describe a posting made with regard to a previous posting of an article. Everyone in the newsgroup can view your follow-up, so be certain of your response! Again, newsreader software will also allow you to send regular e-mail to the writer of a posting. This permits a more private response; and the software will find the e-mail address of the writer for you.

Types of Newsgroups

Newsgroups are topics—many of which may interest you. For anyone over fifty, some of the more important ones are likely to fall under the general headings of finance, health, housing, mobility, and lifestyle.

Newsgroups can be unmoderated or moderated. Unmoderated groups allow for anyone to post a message—relevant or not! Moderated newsgroups involve the intervention of a volunteer who screens postings for relevance, focus, and "goodness of fit." This is important to maintaining the quality of a newsgroup since it keeps out the "quacks" and reduces the volume of information to a manageable level.

Frequently Asked Questions (FAQs) About Newsgroup Topics

To streamline the information-gathering process, many newsgroups compile FAQs, online documents that answer common questions that arise within the newsgroup. It's a good idea to read them before posting a question to the newsgroup. If it's already been addressed in a FAQ you'll likely see a few follow-ups telling you to go and read the FAQ!

Organization of Newsgroups

Because of the large mass of information available, there is a convention for categorizing newsgroups. There are several major global categories, topics, and sub-topics. Nine major newsgroup categories are listed below.

Newsgroup Categories	
rec.	recreational and leisure activities
biz.	business and commercial topics
news.	news and Internet information
soc.	social issues
talk.	topics open to discussion and debate
sci.	scientific topics
comp.	computer-related issues
misc.	other matters (none of the above)
alt.	other alternative, open-ended, and often controversial issues

These are further divided into more topics. For example, the category "rec." may have a topic called gardening or "rec.gardening." Since gardening is a common topic, a sub-topic may exist called "tulip" or "rec.gardening.tulip." You can subscribe to all of the groups within "rec.gardening" (there may be hundreds) or you can fine tune things by subscribing to only "rec.gardening.tulip" (a lot less).

Some Courtesy Tips

The best way to learn the do's and don'ts in USENET is to join some newsgroups and get some information on how to post articles, on how to follow-up, on writing styles, and on other topics. Nothing can replace hands-on experience!

A good reference source is the newsgroup **news.newusers. questions**. You can go there to get a good initial flavour of some of the things you'll need to know about newsgroups.

The Nuts and Bolts of Mailing Lists

Complicating things with a fancy definition of what a mailing list is will, quite frankly, mislead you. A mailing list is just what it sounds like, a process by which documents (mail) is sent to you. The only difference is that it is done electronically on the Internet.

Like newsgroups, mailing lists (often just called a "list") can involve two or two thousand people! And they can cover just about any topic imaginable! After joining one, you will be sent all messages posted to the mailing list through your regular Internet e-mail.

Ease of message creation means that there are lists on just about any topic you can think of. Again, this is why e-mail meets the needs of retirees and near-retirees at least as well as other media. The special needs of retirees are often not addressed or are not easily available through traditional avenues such as books. But because the Internet is so vast and lends itself to specialized topics, you can probably find a "fifty-plus" topic that may not exist in books or in magazines.

Types of Mailing Lists

Mailing lists compile or summarize information. However, there are different ways that such information can be gathered and then presented to you in your e-mail messages. For example, some lists provide simple postings from members about their topic of interest, some summarize information posted in USENET, many post simple announcements and still others are for newsletters. The possible formats are many.

Mailing lists are controlled by different levels of intervention. Some are moderated: a message is screened by an editor who determines whether the message is focussed enough to make it to the mailing list. This may sound a bit intrusive at first, but one of the things that makes mailing lists popular with subscribers is the high quality of content due to an editor's involvement.

Unmoderated lists, on the other hand, permit any message to be sent immediately to all that are on the list. It can be unrestricted, permitting anyone to post to it. Or it can be restricted, permitting only members to post to it.

Subscribing

You can join a mailing list either through e-mail or via Web site subscription. Usually, as you will see in this book, you can subscribe to a mailing list by sending an e-mail message. The text of the message is often in the format "subscribe listname JSmith." Proper format is important since list management software has to be able to interpret it properly. Your e-mail request is usually handled by list management software called a "listserver." This utility automatically adds or deletes your name from the mailing list. You will receive a confirmation of membership and other important information and instructions by e-mail.

It is important to remember to keep this e-mail once you receive it. It usually tells you how to "unsubscribe," or get off of the mailing list when you no longer want to receive its e-mail.

As far as finding a list is concerned, indices may be of help. For example, you can consult the List of Lists at **catalog.com/vivian/interest-group-search.html** to find a mailing list that might meet your needs. This resource is a great way to help you find what you're looking for.

Chapter 3

The Rest and the Best of the Internet

Pioneering Tools of the Net

Telnet

The first time I ever used the Internet, I used a Telnet application, a tool that placed me squarely into the University of Toronto's library system. I remember how convenient this was and how this saved me a trip to the Robarts library when I needed specific information. Today, Internet enthusiasts consider Telnet old news, despite its ability to take you to a library or other resource. This is because the Web offers so much more by way of ease of use, graphics, and general presentability. For example, most of Canada's 3 500 libraries now have Web pages of their own. At these pages, you are offered not only access to text and book indices, but you can also utilize graphics and Web links to community resources.

Nevertheless, Telnet and other older resources such as Gopher, FTP, and Archie still have a place on the Internet—it's just that the underlying documents are retrieved differently. No longer needing separate software applications, these older tools are now superseded by and integrated into the more powerful Web browsers and search tools available today.

Gopher

Gopher is a way to get information that is stored strictly as text files. It allows you to find such information using subject-driven searches of online archives connected to the Internet. For example, if you try to log on to a library, you will likely see a menu which will let you scan offerings from databases such as the library's own collection, the Library of Congress collection, books in print, newspapers, and many other databases of information. All of these sources present text-based information.

You can use your Web browser to access a Gopher site. Just click a hyperlink to a Gopher site if there is one included on a Web site you are viewing. Or, you also can enter a URL in the browser's site location box. Instead of beginning the URL with the http:// prefix reserved for Web sites, you type gopher://.

One site that offers good Gopher primers and provides access points to other Gopher resources can be accessed with your Web browser at **gopher://cwis.usc.edu:70/11/Other_Gophers_and_ Information_Resources/**. At that site you will find a menu of topics, including "How to use Gopher", "Guides to Internet Resources", "Gophers by Subject", "Directories", and more.

Because many Web sites have superseded Gopher resources (or also possess Gopher access links themselves), this book will not focus on these sites. Instead, Web sites, newsgroups, and mailing lists will be the mainstay resources discussed. However, you should know that when you do encounter a Gopher site, it's easy to access it.

FTP (File Transfer Protocol)

FTP is an application that allows for the transfer of files, sounds, graphics, and computer programs from the Internet into your PC.

Like Gopher, FTP can be accessed using most Web browsers. The

URL would start with ftp:// followed by the domain name of the site. Next comes the file directory followed by the file name containing the information you seek.

A note of caution: when downloading anything from the Internet make sure that what you are transferring is free of malicious, file-destroying "viruses." The best way to accomplish this is to obtain anti-virus software, which is available at most software retailers. The extra cost (about $75) is worth it!

If you want more information on FTP, access the Anonymous FTP Frequently Asked Questions (FAQ) List on the Web **www.iaehv.nl/users/perry/ftp-list.html.**

Archie

Archie a tool that allows you to search worldwide data archives by file name. It complements powerful indices such as Yahoo in that it may pick up for you what Yahoo missed. Therefore, Archie is great when you know the name of the file, since it will search various FTP sites from around the world. Use Archie when you know what you want, but don't know where to find it! Otherwise, you should use Yahoo first.

Still Going Strong

Internet Relay Chat (IRC)

One of Hollywood's favourite "computer scenes" is to show an actor "talking" to someone else by keyboard in real time. In other words, they type in comments or questions and get live replies seconds later. This happens in real life too! There is still a very enthusiastic following for this application and it is especially suited to persons who face mobility restrictions but who still wish to interact with others. In a sense, IRC is like a fast version of e-mail!

IRC discussions can be open or private. To use it, you must have IRC software on your PC. You will require an IRC server location (address) to access. Your ISP can help you with locating one (or will provide a list to you). As well, your ISP will help you connect to an IRC server through their own link.

When you are in an IRC "conversation", you log into a "channel," or subject, that is of interest to you. For example, if you key in a phrase or question, all other participants in the channel will view it within seconds. You can then see what they have input in response, thus creating a fully interactive session. But watch out, it's fast. You're simultaneously reading and trying to type in a reply. If hand dexterity is a personal limitation, IRC may not be for you.

You can search for IRC locations ("clients") on any of the Web search engines or go to **www.irchelp.org**.

New Horizons on the Net

Technology moves very quickly, and the way the Internet works changes just as fast. E-mail, the World Wide Web, and newsgroups, in their current general forms, will likely remain the core Internet resources for a while. They combine the immediacy of television or the telephone with the depth of newspapers or magazines. Astoundingly, new technology continues to build upon these already technologically-advanced pillars, sometimes advancing them, sometimes leaving them behind. In the case of Internet originals like Telnet or Archie, new technology has bulldozed and almost replaced them. In other cases, such as the Web or e-mail, new technology has advanced them.

Retirees and near-retirees ought to be beneficiaries of new Internet developments that enhance communication between persons.

While nothing can replace person-to-person contact, technology is making communication faster (e-mail), more interactive (IRC), and more expansive (newsgroups).

Building a Better Mousetrap

The Internet is not only growing in size, it's also growing in quality. The individuals behind existing and new online technology all seek to accomplish one thing—to make the Net easier and more attractive for you to use. This section describes some of the newest bells and whistles in the making!

Access to the Net

Speed-related barriers related to modems are being addressed, as cable Internet connections, 20 to 400 times faster than your typical telephone modems, make it possible to do even more on the Net.

Sound: RealAudio

RealAudio software lets you hear music, radio broadcasts, and more while you are browsing the Web. You can also hear sound while a Web file is in the process of being retrieved. This software can now be easily downloaded from the Internet. Free and priced (which have more bells and whistles than their free counterparts) versions of this software are available through RealAudio's Web site **www.realaudio.com.**

Internet Telephone Calls

A Web link to Australia probably costs about $2 per hour. What would you think of such a rate if a telephone company offered it! Well, if you have a connection to the Internet, appropriate software, speakers, and a small microphone that connects to your PC's sound card, you may be able to make such a call!

Better yet, if you already have the above peripherals, you can sample this technology for free with a software package software called Internet Phone found at **www.vocaltec.com**.

However, calls can only be made between people having similar "phone" software. In addition, the quality of sound is inferior to a telephone and most modems only allow one person to talk at a time. However, effective two-way applications are on their way. Watch for this development.

Video on the Net

More and more Web sites support video files. This means that you can download a video clip and play it on your PC monitor. However, even if you have a fast modem, it could take several minutes to download a 30-second video clip! Nevertheless, once cable or fibre optic Internet hookups become more common, Internet data transfer rates will improve significantly and will allow you to see video in real time. In the meantime, video in multimedia will likely remain the domain of CD ROMs.

Internet Videoconferencing

Internet video-conferencing occurs when persons engage in a live conversation through the Internet while using small video cameras to see each other's faces. This form of communication, previously the stuff of science fiction, is now gaining attention as a potential competitor to the telephone. While currently limited by relatively slow modem speeds, one day it may become the norm. Retirees who are now comfortable with the Internet will be able to reap the benefits of this new way of communicating, especially where their mobility or isolation is an impediment.

Real Time Text and Audio

Real time information, whether based on text or sound, is very popular with Internet users. Stated simply, real time means that there is essentially no wait between the time the information is created and the time it is reported online. Radio is real-time, as is a live TV show. It keeps you up-to-date better than printed matter can.

Virtual Reality

Virtual reality is a development that allows for three-dimensional Web pages. Looking at a sculpture residing in a French museum will never be the same! Computer language to do this is being developed and refined even as you read this book today. Virtual Reality Modeling Language (VRML) is an acronym you'll be hearing more of. It sets the standard for 3D interactive images on the Web. Buck Rogers would be impressed!

Push Technology

Push technology, where content (text, video, and audio) is delivered to you, represents a significant maturing process for the Internet. It recognizes that for every minute spent trying to find information by yourself you lose one minute available for using it.

A new group of Internet players is making push services possible. For now, most applications with push features focus on the delivery of news to you.

And there are also differences between providers of push information. These differences revolve around how they deliver such information and the cost (some are free and some charge for the service). Push provider Web sites will give you a description of their differing services. The table on page 47 lists some popular push information providers.

How can push technology help you? Basically, if you prefer to save time in your leisurely perusal of news, push applications are for you. Also, if you're not sure that your search tools have captured everything you wanted to capture, and you need current information, push is a good alternative information retrieval method.

<table>
<tr><td colspan="2" align="center">**Push Technology Providers**</td></tr>
<tr><td>Castanet Tuner</td><td>**www.marimba.com**</td></tr>
<tr><td>Freeloader</td><td>**www.freeloader.com**</td></tr>
<tr><td>Headliner</td><td>**www.lanacom.com**</td></tr>
<tr><td>MSNBC Personal News Page</td><td>**www.msnbc.com**</td></tr>
<tr><td>My Yahoo News Ticker</td><td>**www.my.yahoo.com**</td></tr>
<tr><td>Netscape In-Box Direct</td><td>**home.netscape.com**</td></tr>
<tr><td>Newsticker</td><td>**www.infomarket.ibm.com**</td></tr>
<tr><td>Pointcast Canada</td><td>**www.pointcast.ca**</td></tr>
<tr><td>The Pointcast Network</td><td>**www.pointcast.com**</td></tr>
</table>

Community Networking

Perhaps one of the most important Internet resources for mature Canadians is the existence of Free-Net or Community Networks. Since most services and programs for retired persons are delivered at the local or provincial levels, it stands to reason that these networks will contain the type of local information that retirees (and anyone over fifty) will be interested in.

The Nuts and Bolts of Free-Net or Community Networks

Mostly non-profit, these networks are usually administered by volunteers from the community. The wide array of services offered often includes limited Internet access, on-line access to local libraries, and participation in local discussion groups.

Not all of these networks are free because of the high cost of administering them. Therefore, some may charge a membership fee, while others will ask for a voluntary donation to help out with the costs.

The Free-Net or Community Network is fed by local providers of information, who are responsible for updating this information periodically. Participants offer information on local programs and events, health services, educational curriculum, legal issues, entertainment, and employment opportunities. Other providers may tell you about their products or services. It is essentially a localized version of the Internet.

To find out more about the Free-Net or Community Network in your area, call the general information line in your county, town, or city hall. They will give you the telephone number of the administrators, who in turn will show you how to log on. You can also find out whether there are fees involved and what the mission of the network is.

New User's Guide Wrap Up

Having read this far, you no doubt know a lot more about the Internet now than you did before. But if you're a new Internet user, you may still be feeling a bit unsure or hesitant about the whole thing. Welcome to the club! Few people will fully grasp the "nuts and bolts" of the Internet on the first read or the first "practice run." And Net-related technology is changing so rapidly that even Internet "experts" struggle in their attempts to fully understand new online developments.

My advice to you? Stick to the basics—at least initially. Read through Part I of this book as slowly and as often as it takes for you to get a good handle on the process of getting "wired" to the Net. You wouldn't be the first person to re-read an Internet-related book. And hands-on practice continues to be an essential ingredient to learning how to use the Net.

When buying a PC, ask the vendor if he will support you in putting it together, and how. Many will be happy to at least provide you with some phone-based assistance. If not, don't worry—ask family, a friend, or a neighbour to help you out. If they also have a PC, they already know how easy it is to set one up. So they'll likely be eager to help you out. What if the PC breaks down? Again, not to worry. Most come with a warranty. A computer industry rule of thumb is that if the PC works on the first try, "out of the box," it will likely work for a lengthy time thereafter. Once you're up and running, just follow the instructions and manuals that come with the PC. Practice really does make perfect!

What about the next step—hooking up to the Net? You read about how to do it; but you may still feel a bit uneasy and tentative about the whole thing. Again, you're not the first to experience these feelings! Ask several ISPs whether they're willing to support your hookup by telephone conversation. Many providers even offer 24-hour support. The industry is so competitive that most will agree to do this. Even when this support is less than "promised," turn to family members and friends for advice and help. Those in the know will demonstrate to you how easy it really is to get connected to the Net. I dare say that an Internet hookup is easier to execute than some camcorder or VCR-to-TV hookups! And be sure to follow the instructions on your browser software. Most are written in concise and easy-to-understand language.

PART II

Mature Canadians and the Internet

Chapter 4

Financial Management on the Web

In this chapter, a series of important financial issues will be presented and discussed. They include:

- Managing Your Bank Accounts on the Web
- Managing Your Investments on the Web
- Your Estate
- Using Internet Resources at Tax Time
- Insurance
- Managing Your Retirement Online
- Government Financial Resources Online

To be sure, these issues are not the exclusive domain of mature Canadians, like yourself. Yet, most people in this stage of life either have a fair amount of financial resources to manage, or are faced with a need to tighten up on their budgets as they leave or prepare to exit the workforce. This chapter will present all of the above issues, and related Internet resources, with a "fifty-plus" perspective.

Managing Your Bank Accounts on the Web

Mature Canadians, more so than their "boomer" counterparts, are typically loyal banking customers. A person that's been in the same neighbourhood for many years and has banked at the corner branch for a long time is not inclined to suddenly change now—at least not unless there's a compelling reason to do so.

However, with government entitlements for older Canadians being pared down, and with the economic pressures that affect us all, perhaps you should re-visit you banking habits. I can assure you that a bank's appreciation of your business will not likely translate into more money in your pocket; and a smile from the bank manager won't help you with the rising cost of living! I'm not necessarily suggesting that you have to change banks. What I am suggesting, however, is that you may wish to change the way you bank—you may want to bank electronically!

My personal advice to those over fifty has always been to avoid debt; and I'm not about to change this personal philosophy now. While the Internet is emerging as a new way to obtain competitive loans, borrowing money is risky business for those Canadians already into the second half of their lives. Thus, discussion in this section (and chapter) will move away from loans and will focus instead on the "savings" side of financial management.

What Is Online Banking?

With the Internet and your PC, you have access to two things. The first is access to information about all financial institutions. You can wield the Internet as a tool to do your financial homework, cut administrative fees, and maximize the returns on your lifelong savings. The second thing you can access is your bank account and other personal financial information. While you can get this information at your branch, it is unlikely that a teller will want to spend the amount of time necessary to get you all the information that you need.

Why Mature Canadians Bank on the Web

You probably know that some banks specialize in servicing the needs of mature Canadians. These branches tend to be located in neighbourhoods where many seniors reside. (Banks do their research well!) Why not access these banks even if such branches are not in your area? All of those "discounts" that target people over fifty ("Seniors' discounts," "60+ discounts," or "50+ discounts") and that reduce banking fees and give you higher yields on GICs and term deposits are accessible online! You can't take advantage of these perks if you don't know about them! How do you find out? You guessed it—through the Net!

With the Internet, you have the ability to locate, assess, and do some comparative shopping on a wide variety of services, financial products, and fees—some especially geared to mature Canadians. Services vary tremendously from bank to bank; more than you may have thought.

The ability to scan the Web pages of different institutions may give you a better "feel" for the services they offer or the expertise they possess. Printed descriptions on Web pages tend to be more accurate than information given to you over the phone by a rushed or misinformed employee. Perhaps, as a mature Canadian, you are now ready for the types of specialized services offered by trust companies? Maybe it is estate issues that matter to you most, now that your children are grown up and other "fifty-plus" issues are cropping up and need to be dealt with. While banks are selling just about everything these days, some institutions simply do a better job at something like estate planning than others. The Internet helps you find them.

The ritual of walking or driving into a wintry, sub-zero Canadian snowstorm is an experience that most people like to avoid. While nothing can replace a healthy walk to the bank or inter-personal contact (something I stress throughout this book), why not use online banking as an additional way of doing from home what you've always done before—banking.

You may have built up a substantial nest egg or may only possess a modest one. Either way, you want to be sure that your life savings are protected. You've heard a little about the Canada Deposit Insurance Corporation (CDIC), offering $60 000 maximum protection; but did you know that there are ways to double-up on this protection? Did you know that not all financial instruments are protected? Many mature Canadians do not. An online visit to CDIC at **www.cdic.ca/** is a lot easier than phoning through the maze of voice-mail that is typical of many "information lines." At the CDIC site, you can access information on how your savings are (or can be) protected from loss.

Most significantly, a key reason why you, a mature Canadian, may want to consider banking online is the fact that more and more financial institutions are allowing all customers to access the details of their bank accounts electronically, anytime and anywhere. Secure Internet transactions are already available, making interactive banking a current reality. Security software is getting better all the time. In fact, most persons agree that there is now a lower risk of fraud to you through the Net than say, having someone look at your credit card number (or take your duplicate credit card slip) in a store and use it for fraudulent purposes. Nevertheless, before setting up an interactive bank account, get informed by the bank as to security and coverage for loss.

So re-evaluate the basis of your current banking habits. Stay with a bank only if it provides you with appropriate discounts, and the best returns on savings available to mature customers. In summary, the Internet changes the way you approach the management of your own finances. Instead of simply being a longstanding, passive bank customer, you are now empowered to actively deposit, change, or withdraw your funds by yourself. Also, you're a well-educated customer at that!

Interactive Banks in Canada. Is Anyone Home?

While all banks now have an Internet presence, not all are up to speed or can claim to be advanced Internet "converts." The most fundamental test to apply to bank Web sites is to ask "Is anyone home?" In other words, are the bells and whistles of bank Web sites supported by actual, informed people on the other side? Before choosing to bank on the Web—especially if "banking" to you means accessing and altering your bank accounts and balances—phone a few of the numbers on their sites. Do you actually get through to live and knowledgeable people? Are you bounced to the "information" line—an endless maze of voice mail? When I applied this test to one particular bank, I was transferred to the main switchboard three times where I spoke to three different people, and was put on hold for twenty minutes during that time. My question was never answered. Despite this, I believe in two things: (i) that financial institutions will learn the importance of good Web site support, and (ii) that in the meantime, the information already on their sites is indeed very useful. Let us now take a closer look at some of the resources.

Banking Information on the Web

Banking information is one form of "financial" information. Financial information encompasses not only banking, but investment, estate, tax, and insurance matters. These are discussed in separate sections in this chapter, where many advisory and educational resources are presented. Banking information, on its own, deals with personal finances, product and service fees, special services for seniors, monitoring interest rates and the economy, calculating future payments/receipts, and so on. It's everything you consider traditional banking, except now it's available online. The TD Bank's home page (**www.tdbank.ca**) typifies comprehensive online banking services in Canada.

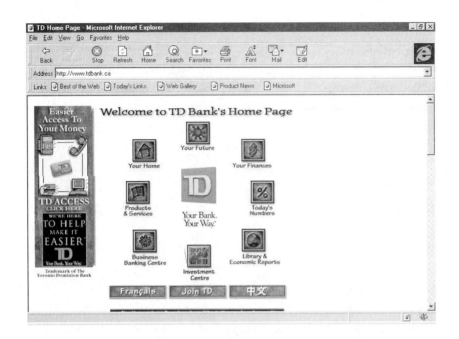

What's Their Address?

When looking for the "address" (URL) of a bank's, trust company's, or credit union's Web site, you can access Yahoo's financial services directory at **www.yahoo.com/Business_and_Economy/ Companies/Financial_Services/Banking/Directories**. Once there, enter the name of the bank you seek. Or, using your available selection of linked search engines, you can enter keywords such as personal finance, banking services, and financial services and Yahoo will assemble a list of sites for you. Once you've found the bank Web site, you will notice that the best ones provide locators (directories) of their branches and services. Also note that a similar, more "international" financial institution directory can be accessed at Ibanker (**www.ddsi.com/banking**).

How Does Online Bank Information Differ?

Web content, or banking information, varies from bank to bank. Banks such as the TD Bank and the Royal Bank have Web page after Web page of facts and figures on topics such as financial services and products, domestic economic data, global interest rates, recent press releases, and more. Others are not so advanced. But one thing is sure, their Web page content will change periodically. It is this currentness of information that makes their Web page content valuable to you. Also, easy access to information is important, especially if restricted mobility is an issue with you.

Many banks are also providing online banking services. This means that you can access your account with your PC. You can pay bills, transfer funds, get a statement, manage investments, and verify balances through your PC. If you've moved to a retirement villa or now live full-time at your cottage in your retirement years, you know how convenient this could be.

So as you can see, some banks provide non-interactive Web content only, some have content and interactive online banking, and others have neither—yet.

PC versus Internet Banking

Not all interactive banking services are created equal. One system of online banking is called "PC (direct-dial/private network) banking." In this system you use your modem and computer, but you dial the bank directly, you don't use the Internet. The other system is Web-based banking over the Internet. PC banking may be more palatable to those over fifty, who tend to be more "cautious" about emerging technologies than their younger counterparts—especially when lifetime savings are involved! The end result, however, is very similar—efficient and informed banking.

PC Banking and Web Banking: The Players
Providers of PC ("private network") banking include the CIBC (**www.cibc.com/online**), TD Bank (**www.tdbank.ca**), and Canada Trust (**www.canadatrust.com**).

Providers of full or partial (that is, not all services are online) Web banking include Scotiabank (**www.scotiabank.com**), the Royal Bank (**www.royalbank.com**), and Vancouver City Savings Credit Union (**www.vancity.com**). Mbanx (**www.mbanx.com**), for example, allows customers to bank by phone, PC (Web), or facsimile—in Canada or in the U.S. The phone banking option is useful for snowbirds, who may feel isolated from their financial affairs "back home."

What Exactly Am I Looking for Online?

The best Web sites allow you to take something back, usually valuable information. TD Bank's Budget Guide (**www.tdbank. ca/tdbank/pers/guide/retire.html**) is especially suited for those in their 50s, 60s, 70s, or even 80s. Because retiree or near-retiree cash flows tend to be predictable (for example the proposed Seniors Benefit and CPP payments) this resource is even more relevant to you. The TD Bank's Retirement Planning link provides an online calculator that helps you establish a "retirement budget." This tool will help you better control your long-term finances. Financial planners charge fees for this service. You can get it for free on the Net. Many other financial Web resources provide "budget calculators." Look for them. They're user-friendly, so long as you enter in the correct amounts, and can save you money—consultant-wise and cash control-wise.

The best "fifty-plus" financial institution Web sites will provide you with more information than you used to be able to get before online banking was an option. In addition, they usually promote reduced service fees for older Canadians. Look for such sites and such arrangements. Preferential savings rates are also given to those who deposit large sums of cash. Retirees, or near retirees who, in many cases, have accumulated substantial savings throughout their lifetimes, will find Internet rate searches invaluable. In some cases, the savings achieved through proper research will essentially pay for the cost of your PC! Learn about financial products and services offered to get a "feel" for an institution. Finally, decide which institution is best for your special needs. A newly-discovered bank or trust company that is sensitive to these needs should be at least as acceptable to you as your current one. Be a vigilant consumer. It's your savings that are at stake!

Don't just consider the size of a financial institution. The Internet is universal, allowing for large and small participants. As long as you have CDIC or equivalent protection, consider smaller Canadian banks, foreign institutions operating in Canada, and local credit unions. Mature Canadians are used to a personal touch and want to feel that the persons behind Web sites are accessible. Other Canadians, perhaps of Chinese origin, may prefer service in their own language. The Hongkong Bank of Canada (**www.hkbc.ca**) and the TD Bank (**www.tdbank.ca**) sites both excel at addressing the international finance and language needs of much of their clientele—recognizing that many potential customers are multi-lingual, over fifty, and far from technophobic!

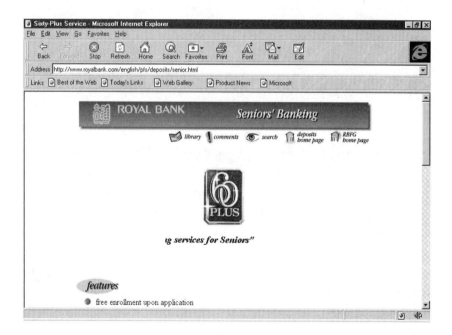

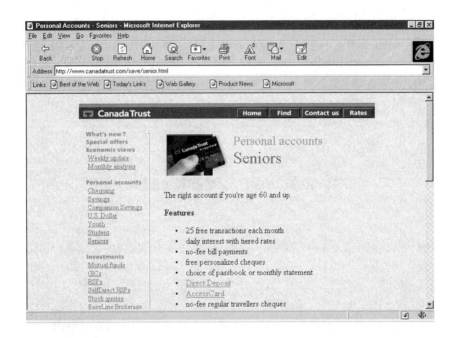

To Change or Not to Change—That Is the Question

As a mature Canadian, you've likely developed a banking relationship with your bank manager. Don't underestimate the value of such a relationship. Send him or her an e-mail if you have a question. Cultivate such contact. On the other hand, many banks rotate their managers to curtail such relationships. If banks can do this, why can't you?

My advice as to whether to switch banks (that is, just switch banks without going online, or switch banks and bank online at the new one) depends on your general financial situation. If you're in your 50s and still have some debt to pay off, it may be wise to stay where you are. Your branch knows you and your good payment habits. Even if you're paying more in interest than you would otherwise pay elsewhere, weigh this against the benefit of a good existing banking relationship. Don't expose yourself to unnecessary tests of creditworthiness.

If you're debt-free, you're less dependent on a banking relationship. In fact, the bank should be going out of its way to serve you. In this case, be adventurous. Educate yourself about banks and consider your options. You don't even have to embrace online banking. But as a minimum, consider changing banks if your research, made easier by the Net, points you to this course of action.

Managing Your Investments on the Web

Persons over fifty have never been in as much of a financial quandary as they are today. Near-historic low interest rates are being applied on their savings accounts, GICs, and term deposits. It's getting to the point that they're almost being forced out of fixed-return investments. The stock market beckons in turn. News and ads about mutual funds are fed daily to potential customers by print and by TV. The possibility of a major stock market correction hangs over investors' heads like a sword. What do these Canadians do? What do you do?

GICs and term deposits may have served you well in the past when rates were higher. And maybe you never really intended to learn any more about investments. You depended on "professional" financial advice. But even advisory fees are now eating away into your savings, slowly, unnoticeably, but nonetheless gnawing away.

If there's one area of the Internet where the saying "knowledge is power" rings true, it's the area of investments. Think about it. Markets rise and fall based on news on the economy, an industry, or even a big company. If you had information on what most "experts" think will happen to interest rates at the next U.S. Federal Reserve Bank meeting, and you know that stock markets experience turbulence when rates rise suddenly, you can make an "educated", temporary move out of the stock market until actual data is released or until things settle down.

In many cases, investment information emanates from credible sources such as Bloomberg (**www.bloomberg.com**). In other cases, information from resources such as Web-based discussion forums or newsgroups has to be taken with a healthy dose of scepticism. The table below provides general guidelines on judging the quality of investment Web pages. The concepts found there can also be adapted to apply to newsgroups, mailing lists, and even some non-investment Web sites. Therefore, keep these five general points in mind and apply them to other resources discussed in this book. They are important—your finances are at stake!

Checklist for Investment Web Pages

Correctness	Are information sources clearly listed?
	Is responsibility for the information clearly presented?
	Are graphs and financial charts easy to read (an indicator of quality and diligence)?
Authority	Is the publisher of the Web page financial information credible?
	Who is sponsoring the page?
	Are Web publisher qualifications stated?
	Are telephone numbers or e-mail addresses provided?
Objectivity	Is the content of the financial page presented free of bias?
	Is the tone of information presentation factual or opinionated?
Currentness	Are page dates provided to show first publication and last update?
	Does it look up-to-date?

Depth and Breadth	Are financial topics discussed in sufficient detail on which to base a financial decision?
	If the page is a component of a larger written or online piece, is the location of that source piece provided?

In this section, investment-related Web resources will be presented. Special attention will be drawn to Web resources that meet the special investment needs of those over fifty. These resources tend to deal with safer fixed-term investments, mutual funds, preferred shares, and hybrids of the above.

What Kind Information Is Out There?

The next table provides a list of the kinds of information that can be accessed on the Internet. The cost? For the most part, nil. In other cases, specialized information comes with a fee. But for most people, this free Internet information rivals and exceeds the quality and quantity of "pre-Net" information available from financial institutions.

Types of Investment Information on the Internet

stock quotes	SEC documents (Form 10-Ks)
stock graphs and charts	trading services
mutual fund prospectuses	bond advice
initial public offerings	press releases
E-zines	push news delivered to you
corporate news	(e.g. Pointcast)
futures/options quotes	company bulletins
electronic newspapers	personal opinions (newsgroups
databases (searchable)	and online forums)

Educating Yourself on the Net

Starting Out

As you can see from the previous table, your information choices are boundless. What's more, your choices within each category of investment information are even more plentiful. So where do you start?

If you already know a lot about the different types of investments out there and consider yourself to be a sophisticated investor, start with **www.yahoo.com**, the Yahoo directory. From the main menu, go to "business and economy." Once there, go to "markets and investments." Faced with still more sub-directories, each with a search button, you can now do a more narrowed search for what you're looking for. In addition, this section of the chapter will provide you with Web addresses of some of the more sophisticated investment Web sites.

But what if you're a novice in the investment area and want to learn more about the various types of investments available in the marketplace? For example, what's a "derivative instrument?" Can Yahoo help you find out? After all, Yahoo gives you a comprehensive list of investment information. Certainly, you can find it there! The problem with directories such as Yahoo is that they probably won't inform you as to what specific investments really do or who they are best for. Yahoo only points you to sites. Therefore, you'll still need a bit more help.

Investment Basics

If you're new to investments, or simply want to know more about them, go to several of the Web's "Investment Glossaries" discussed below. In addition, investment-related guides and FAQs are also available on the Internet and can assist you in your quest for basic investment information. The educational information available is balanced—not so much that you are overwhelmed, yet not so little that you're under-informed. You want simple, useful information. You also want to minimize risk.

The Bre-X debacle is a prime example of how risky investments can get. Even in a "connected" world, investors still had to wait one month for a verdict on Bre-X's gold reserves. It's a prime example of why pre-investment research is critical. Many investors jumped into this stock when it was high, basing their decision on sensational news reporting. They thought that Bre-X (a junior mining company) was the same type of business operation as Barrick Gold (one of the most established mining companies in the world). Had they done basic research, they would have realized that many start-ups like Bre-X usually start off in the "red." They're loaded with debt and risk.

Again, an investment glossary is a good "first step" resource to help you better understand the world of stocks, bonds, and mutual funds. Data Broadcasting Corporation's site (**www.dbc. com/cgi-bin/htx.exe/newsroom/glossary.htm**) provides such information. Or, if you wish, enter the terms "investment glossary" into Yahoo, or any other Web directory, which will generate a list of other available glossaries that provide quick explanations of complex terms.

The Securities and Exchange Commission (SEC) (**www.sec. gov/consumer/weisktc.htm**) is another credible and authoritative stop-off point for educating yourself. Investment basics are covered there in good depth and breadth.

If you seek information about mutual funds, the Financial Post (**www.canoe.ca/Money/primer_mutual.html**) provides an overview of this investment vehicle. A related resource is the Investment Funds Institute of Canada (**www.mutfunds.com/ific**). Newsgroups such as **misc.invest** or **misc.invest.funds**, while not as authoritative, can provide you with an "investors" perspective.

Bond primers on the Net are few and far between. However,

most of the "information about mutual funds" resources referred to above also contain good discussion about the types of secure bonds out there—government, utility, corporate, etc. For more basic Canada Savings Bond (CSB) information, the Bank of Canada's CSB site (**www.bank-banque-canada.ca/csb-oec/ csbae.htm**) has a CSB overview, current rate information, and a bond value calculator. Their home page can also guide you to their "Publications," their "Library," or their "Currency Museum" pages. The provinces also offer bonds. For example, Ontario bonds are delivered by the province's Ministry of Finance. The general search principle here is to go the provincial home page and directory (such as **www.gov.on.ca** for Ontario) and from there click on more links until you reach Finance and the bond-related page(s). (URLs for provincial government sites are presented in the "Government Financial Resources Online" section at the end of this chapter.)

If you seek GIC or term deposit (TD) information, the best sources to go to are the providers of GIC or TD products—the banks and trust companies, as discussed in the previous section.

Your Investor Profile

Many persons over fifty have built up enough savings to enable them to put a certain portion towards riskier investments—stocks, options, and derivatives of those. For these individuals even losing money on these investments would not impact significantly on their retirement lifestyle. Others cannot afford to take any financial risk and cannot absorb significant losses. Still others are in between these extremes. Which investments (such as mutual funds) are best for all of these circumstances?

Guidelines to help you answer this question can be found at **www.banksite.com/pmf1.htm**, Banksite's "Investor Profile" page.

At this site, you can take a "risk tolerance" quiz. Based on your score and risk preference, you can see which types of investments are best for you.

Obtaining Information about Companies and Their Shares

Now that you're knowledgeable about the investment industry you can get start to gather information about specific companies. As a graduate of (or long-time alumni) of "investment school," you can use the Web to access all sorts of company information.

Words and Numbers

A perfect example of what a good Web site looks like can be found at Silicon Investor (SI) at **www.techstocks.com**. Geared at its inception to technology companies, this Web resource now tracks publicly traded companies in other industries. Canadian exchanges are accessible too. It is more interactive and more powerful than anything you can find on even most brokers' Web sites.

At Silicon Investor, you can chart a stock's performance (price and volume) on a weekly, monthly, or yearly basis. You can get quotes that are updated every few minutes. Its interactivity is best exemplified in its Stock Talk pages, where you can follow or participate in discussion threads. But watch out for misinformation. Treat what you read with a healthy dose of scepticism. Act on good information (as discussed previously). This site has really caught on quickly with investors and is the largest in its class.

Comparable SI-wannabe sites include Investools (**www. investools.com**) and Stockmaster (**www.stockmaster.com**).

Distinctly Canadian sites include Canada Stock Watch (**www. canada-stockwatch.com**). At this site you can get TSE (and NYSE)

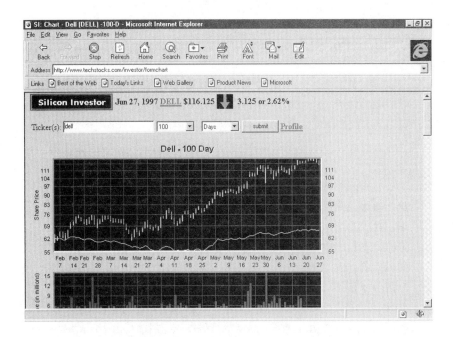

price and volume charts as well as company information. There is a small charge (49 cents +) for company bulletins. Canada News Wire (**www.newswire.ca**) also provides you with recent press releases of Canadian companies and organizations.

You can also access the annual reports of companies by going directly to their home pages and by locating their annual report links. Use your browser's search features (or use other search engines like WebCrawler) to get to a public company's home page. If their annual reports are in Adobe Acrobat mode (where what you would see in a printed report is what you get through your PC), and you haven't downloaded the Adobe Acrobat software yet, you can download this program for free into your PC. How to do this is usually explained on the very page where you discovered you needed the software. Many companies have "financial" Web pages containing all kinds of investment-related information. But be sure to look at the source of this information carefully. Was it audited or otherwise certified? Does it look biased? Due diligence on your part is important anytime you act on Internet information—especially when it has financial impact.

Words from the Wise

Dave Johnston (**johnston@mulberry.com**) of Ottawa cites lots of benefits of the Internet, not the least of which were investment-related.

> *The benefits of the Internet to 50+ people are innumerable! It brings the whole world into your own home. You can use it as you need or desire. It brings you information about all aspects of health, travel, hobbies, and, of course, investment.*
>
> *I, along with numerous other older people whom I know, enjoy checking our investments regularly via Internet; it gives them great satisfaction and control of their finances. My entire family use the Web, e-mail, and newsgroups almost daily. The Internet is a very active part of our home operation.*

Johnson recommends a hands-on learning approach. "In the computer area, you have unlimited friends; make use of their help," adds Johnson.

John Ripley (**jripley@island.net**) of Nanaimo, B.C., Canada, also has some advice in this area.

> *I have been semi-retired for over a year and have found that the Internet allows me to do something I have always wished for—to be able to closely monitor the stock market without having to phone my broker every day. I can view the market action right on my monitor. I pay a monthly fee for "real time" (no delay) updates. News releases are accessible as they become released and com-*

pany data, charts for up to 3 years, trading history, and previous news releases are available for all Canadian stocks at **canstock.com.**

There are many free investment services as well. I have bookmarked [saved the URLs in a section of the browser so that they're easier to return to] about 80 so far. One that I use daily to print the end of market results for my active stocks is **quotes.galt.com.**

A word of advice: be wary of investment forums (discussion threads on a company), as many individuals use this media to affect the price on stocks they own. And never risk your retirement funds on the stock market (especially penny stocks). All stocks go up and down, and some collapse. So treat it as entertainment and only risk money you could afford to lose. Spend weeks or months to get informed and connected to good info sources on the Net before you start investing. It can fill your days if you so desire.

General Advice—Newsletters, Newspapers, and Journals

The value of Web-based publications (online newsletters, newspapers, and journals) resides in the fact that they not only present data (plain facts, figures, and graphics), but they also provide general, non-personal, useful information on which you yourself can base decisions. It's a little more than just getting simple quotes; and a little less than what you get when you visit a financial advisor or broker. So you can ask yourself—"I get this with my paper. Why do I need the Net?" The main advantage with the Internet is that you can access specialized information that doesn't normally make it to print. Also, you can access industry experts. This is especially true of newsletters, which will be discussed momentarily.

The Wall Street Journal (WSJ) is a definitive, international-scope investment publication—and it's available online (**www.wsj.com**). Because it's a newspaper (albeit an electronic one), you'll have to pay an annual subscription fee. If you're retired up in the Laurentians, you know hard it is to get an American paper. For the sophisticated investor, it's a resource to consider. I'm always amazed to see how a good or bad WSJ article on a particular company affects its stock price on the same day; more so than any other paper. The Globe and Mail, another investment-oriented newspaper, can be browsed at **www.globeandmail.com** for similar Canadian fee-based services. At this site, you can also access Report on Business Magazine online.

For more Canadian-oriented content, the Canadian Stock Market Reporter (CSMR) (**www.canstock.com**) is a good bet. There is a fee, but a free trial subscription is offered. There, you can browse recent news releases and old news archives. In addition, "insider trading" reports are accessible by subscribers. For American content and similar services, try Market Guide (**marketguide.com**), CSMR's US counterpart.

For the very sophisticated, there's Telenium Services (**www. telenium.ca**), where you can obtain a wealth of stock, mutual fund, futures, options, and derivative financial instrument information. It is strong on the "business reporting" side of things, as business news and general financial advice can be found at this site.

In terms of newsletters, one of the foremost Canadian authorities on mutual funds and the financial markets in general is Gordon Pape, well-known author and "Web publisher." His site (**www.gordonpape.com**) provides access to his newsletters and books—his general advice. In addition to providing ratings of mutual funds, Pape's site has useful links to mutual fund company pages and other financial destinations. Again, this is another site that is strong on "business reporting."

As for my advice, make sure you have researched the credibility of any online publication before acting on its underlying advice. Some you will have heard about; others will be obscure. The key here is research. Make sure the source is good, again by following the guidelines outlined above, and by applying simple common sense.

Online Advisors

Online advice refers to direct (usually e-mail-driven) advice provided by individuals to individuals. It's essentially personal advice by computer. Online advice does not generally refer to Internet newsletters provided by banks, trust companies, or well-known authorities for the benefit of individuals. While still scarce, online advisory services are expected to grow, as investment advisors turn to the Internet to ply their trade.

I don't recommend that anyone over fifty act on online advice provided by individuals—unless they are proven professionals and known authorities in the investment field. Simply stated, the online medium is too risky and e-mail investment advice is unnecessary. It's risky because your life savings are at stake and there may be unseen, anonymous scam artists on the Net, especially where money is so obviously involved. It's unnecessary because the same advice can be obtained in person or by other more conventional means.

The best course of action for you to follow is to stick with the experts; proven and professional financial planners and advisors who are trained and experienced at providing investment advice. Getting such advice requires personal contact—the advisor has to know your circumstances!

One large brokerage company that can provide you with personal as well as online investment advice is Midland Walwyn (**www.midwal.ca**). Their "financial tips" pages allow you to access this week's and prior weeks' online financial and investment advice. Also, you can browse through their comprehensive menu of investor services.

Midland Walwyn can also be accessed through CARP's site. You may want to consider entering through this "back door." This is because a unique series of Web pages has been created solely for the benefit of Fifty-Plus.Net visitors. What's so beneficial about these pages? Firstly, Midland Walwyn offers service discounts to CARP members. It also offers them free seminars. And, if you don't wish to become a member, but nevertheless require basic "fifty-plus" financial information, you can still take advantage of this site. For example, you can access a main menu pointing you to Midland Walwyn financial service information, their special estate and Seniors Benefit reports, a local directory of their financial advisors, and even a chat line where you can pose an investment-related question. This site has aligned itself specifically as a "fifty-plus" site and is definitely useful to mature Canadian's concerned about their finances. To get to these Web pages, access Fifty-Plus.Net (**www.fifty-plus.net**) and click on the Midland Walwyn icon.

Once you have educated yourself, researched companies, monitored quotes, and read the mainstream investment publications—as described in this section—you have the basic tools needed for the next step: the trade.

Online Trading

The TD Bank's introduction of WebBroker in 1997 (**webbroker. greenline.ca**) heralded a revolution in discount online trading services in Canada. Online Internet trading allows individuals to manage their own investment portfolios—through their PC. At WebBroker, you can place buy and sell orders for North American options and equities, you can get account information, and you can obtain real-time quotes on the Internet. The Hongkong Bank of Canada's Internet discount trading arm (**www.hkbc.ca**) also provides online Internet trading services.

Expect online Internet trading (like online banking) to grow in the next few years, following the growth in popularity of telephone-based discount trading when it was introduced years ago.

Finally, if you like trading but prefer to use "Monopoly" money, try the InvestLink site (**www.investlink.com**) where, in addition to accessing real annual reports and quotes, you can select a dream portfolio. Later, you can monitor its performance to see how you would have done had you invested real money. With the markets being the fickle creatures that they are these days, this may be the only healthy way to invest!

Your Estate

Mature Canadians need to consider their mortality. Facing this reality means that there are important family, spiritual, and financial issues to address. The process of dealing with end-of-life financial issues is called "arranging (or planning) your estate."

You need to determine what will happen to your financial and other assets after you die. Do you have to eliminate some debt first? Do you have enough insurance to cover existing and future liabilities and still have money left over for your loved ones? Will the tax man hit hard, or is there anything you can do to minimize taxes? These are some of the typical issues addressed in the estate planning process.

Many Canadians wait too long to deal with estate planning issues. Simply stated, it's not fun, it takes time, it's difficult to do, and it usually costs money. However, consider the long-term benefits of proper planning—your family won't get stuck with long delays, red-tape, legal costs, and personal turmoil in receiving your bequest.

Because it's difficult to arrange your estate, you may need help from banks, trust companies, financial planners, lawyers, and accountants. Do you see the dollar signs already?

While the Net cannot replace the personal, face-to-face advice of a professional who knows exactly what your personal circumstances and needs are, getting a head start by doing some research on the Internet can help you make better decisions and, as importantly, can help you keep estate administration costs down.

A Step by Step Overview

The Internet has valuable, informative Web resources that can take you through the estate management process step by step. Most online resources, however, only provide information about components of this process. It's up to you to piece the detail together into a "big picture." For example, a lawyer may have a great Web site on preparing a will. An accountant may have a strong site on minimizing taxes on death. And an insurance company may have all you need to know about seniors' insurance. Get the picture—the "big picture" to be exact?

To help you make sense of this puzzle, I will present a brief and general overview to as to what the "big picture" of managing your estate is all about. Then, you can access relevant Internet resources for the components of this whole—tax Web sites, legal Web sites, and related Internet resources.

In my first book—*Ontario Retirement Handbook* (ECW Press)—
I detailed the steps involved in arranging one's estate. These are
generic steps, pertinent to all Canadians. Selected highlights
follow.

Know What You Own, Know What You Owe Sound easy? You would
be surprised what people miss when asked "What do you own?"
Just ask an estate planning specialist! She will tell you that this
is one of the biggest hurdles for her clients to overcome. Last
minute calls abound from clients who forget to tell their estate advisors about that insurance policy with a high cash surrender
value or about that hidden debt. It throws off the planner's cal-
culations in a big way. This oversight, in turn, often results in a
higher fee for you.

So write down the names and locations of cash and investments, real
estate, insurance policies, pension plans (private or group), receiv-
ables (business or personal), personal property (cars, jewellery,
etc.), and personal liabilities (lines of credit, mortgages, stock mar-
gin accounts, etc.). Keep this information up-to-date and accessible.

Know Who Gets What Avoid potential family turmoil that sometimes arises when it's not clear who'll get your cottage or your
stamp collection. Nothing is worse than unnecessary tension during what is already a difficult time.

To avoid confusion, consider equal, portion-based, dollar-based,
or specific item bequests. A mix of the above can also work well
for you and your beneficiaries.

Death and Taxes After you die, your executor will be legally compelled to prepare a tax return deeming many of your assets to
be disposed of. Your estate will be taxed on any gains that may
arise from deemed dispositions. What can you do? A lot! Central
to reducing your estate-related taxes is knowing who gets what,
as described above. However, it gets tricky because what you

want to give to someone may not be what is ultimately best vis-à-vis tax reduction on death. It's a balancing act between personal, net cash flow, and tax issues. Preliminary advice is required—advice that can be found on the Internet.

Enter the accountants and tax lawyers! Many of these professionals have started to advertise through the Web. They often provide useful, relevant information on their site, and list the ancillary services they offer. Ernst and Young's Web site (**www. eycan.com/tax**) has online publications on tax issues and is worth a visit. KPMG, another large firm with a solid Internet presence (**www.kpmg.ca/tax**), has even more extensive online tax information.

Don't forget the search engines either. Try keying in some keywords like "tax tips" or "estate planning"—you'll be surprised at what's out there. Rollovers, estate freezes, and other tools of the tax trade can be read about on the Net. Don't go overboard, however. Just get the basic facts. Ultimately, you want to know what the advice is all about when your personal tax advisor gives you a recommendation.

Executor, Not Executioner Most people think of an executor (the administrator of your estate) as someone who has to coldly do the "dirty work" of settling an estate. This person is also commonly perceived to be someone that is supposed to be suited to the tedium involved: government red tape and endless phone calls. These perceptions could not be further from the truth!

While it's true than the executor(s) you select should be impartial and reasonably adept at financial issues, it is equally important that he be sensitive to your wishes, your family circumstances, and other intangibles.

Where will you find your executor if you don't have one yet? Is the one you already appointed the ideal candidate after all? A good executor will, in many cases, be a trusted friend, family member, or former business partner. Trust companies and banks offer executorial services, but my advice is to first find someone "closer to home," someone who is financially and otherwise competent, and trustworthy. If the well runs dry there, try a qualified financial planner. The key is to make sure they know (or are likely to learn quickly) your personal situation. I don't recommend that you appoint someone you don't really know, such as someone you encountered through the Web. But if you are determined to find someone through the Web, go to the larger banks and trust companies where you'll likely be getting advice from someone who is properly trained.

Write Your Will My disdain for will and power of attorney (POA) kits (costly, pre-formatted, "paint-by-number" legal documents that attempt to simplify very complex issues) is amplified as I observe that more and more of these are being sold through the Net. There are several reasons why you should avoid will and POA kits.

Firstly, you can usually get free will-preparation advice from many community legal services or clinics. Secondly, many provincial Public Trustee offices offer POA kits free of charge. Lastly, and most importantly, will kits give people a false comfort that their estate is taken care of. Few kits remind you of the other "big picture" estate arrangement steps that need to be taken. Not only are you paying for something that can otherwise be obtained for free, you also run the risk of costly errors and oversights down the road. It's not the "paper" part of your will that matters. It's the advice or content within it that counts!

As a bare minimum, your will should address the following areas.

- A designation of your executor(s),
- Clear instruction as to how your monetary assets, personal use assets, and other bequests should be distributed, and

- Provision for your executor to take advantage of any tax breaks allowed under Canadian tax law.

Keep your will (existing or new) up-to-date. Why? To adapt to changing circumstances such as the death of a beneficiary (such as your spouse), divorce, new grandchildren, or even re-marriage. Estate planning, especially as it pertains to wills, involves complex issues. So make sure that your advisor is competent, qualified, and well-spoken of.

Advice on Advice

Seek professional advice when planning your estate, even after you've browsed the Web for preliminary background information. Nothing replaces a personal touch and good advice in this important area.

Online Information on Arranging Your Estate

As with any other financial issue discussed in this chapter, a critical first step is for you to get informed. To this end, banks and trust companies provide most of the Web resources in the estate planning area. In addition to information on tax, executor, and will-related issues, many financial institution Web sites also provide detailed information on setting up trusts as part of the estate management process.

The TD Bank's Estate Planning pages (**www.tdbank.ca/tdbank/ifepl/estate/index.html**) typify what similar sites offer by way of online estate planning information. This site does a good job of integrating all of the components of the estate planning process into one stop. It provides a planning approach, trust information, power of attorney tips, executor selection criteria, and will-preparation advice. It's comprehensive and convenient, arming you with some relevant knowledge before you hand over your valuable estate administration business to someone!

Many financial institutions have search tools and indices on their Web pages. Enter key words such as "estate planning" or "trusts" to locate the right pages. And, there's always Yahoo!

Using Internet Resources at Tax Time

Like death, taxes cannot be avoided or evaded. But the sting of taxes can be minimized! And although you may be thinking about your mortality a little bit more than before, you need not think as often about taxes. That's because Revenue Canada (RevCan), and other taxation "players" have jumped on the Internet, and that's made tax time a lot easier.

Multiple Choices

While filling out a tax return by hand is the approach most frequently used by Canadian taxpayers, alternatives are emerging and are gaining in popularity. For example, the availability of tax return preparation software and electronic filing (E-file) to Revenue Canada has made the tax return filing process a little faster—especially when used the second time around. But speed is only one part of the complete tax puzzle. Another more important part is the accurate planning of your financial affairs to minimize your taxes. Enter the Net.

Your first "learning" step is getting informed as to your rights as a taxpayer. Even if, in the end, you have someone else actually prepare or E-file your tax return for you, there's a wealth of information on the Net that you should get well-acquainted with first. The Internet delivers the tax information you need—without the wait, the endless reading, the aggravation, or the hefty fees. Don't just hand over your tax affairs to someone blindly. First, acquire at least a basic understanding of essential tax principles— something that is especially easy to do on the Net!

Revenue Canada

RevCan's pages (**www.revcan.ca/Emenu.html**) are filled with information: guides, publications, technical papers, brochures, and forms related to just about every Canadian tax issue in existence. For example, if you run a business from home, you can access the most current payroll deduction formulae. These can even be transferred right into your payroll calculation software. You can also access Web pages that deal with trusts and your general rights as a taxpayer. Also, if you're missing a certain tax form such as the T1C Seniors form and don't want to hear RevCan's busy signal or worse—wait in line at one of their offices—then pay their site a visit. You can download tax forms with relative ease.

Despite the abundance of RevCan's online resources, however, you still can't actually do your tax return on the Net. That's because RevCan wants to be absolutely sure that the Net is secure. Residing in one document, a tax return contains the single biggest collection of sensitive personal information imaginable. RevCan (or its army of conservative accountants) can't be blamed for waiting to see if something bad happens to "the other guy" first— can they?

Accounting firms

Four of the larger accounting firms, KPMG (**www.kpmg.ca**), Deloitte & Touche (**www.dtonline.com** or **www.deloitte.ca**), Ernst & Young (**www.eycan.com**), and Coopers and Lybrand (**www.ca.coopers.com**), all maintain Web sites that can help you plan and prepare your taxes. Their information and advice can save money and clarify complex tax issues for you. It seems that the larger the firm, the more complete its Web resources are. Their online help is available in various areas.

Home-Based Business Advice

If you are supplementing your regular income with business income, there are a variety of ways (deductions, carry-forwards, deferrals, credits, etc.) to reduce your overall taxes. Browse KPMG's site at **www.kpmg.ca**. There you will find tips on identifying and claiming allowable business expenses to reduce tax.

RRSP Advice

Feel a need to top up that RRSP before full retirement? Visiting **www.eycan.com/tax/tax.htm** at Ernst & Young will allow you to calculate the taxes saved at various RRSP contribution levels while you are online.

Travelling to the U.S.

KPMG's Snowbirds Tax Page (**snowbird.kpmg.ca**) has the information you may need to determine whether you are liable for U.S. residency tax. The site prompts you for the length of stay and a few other details and then provides you with some quick but important answers. Deloitte's site (**www.deloitte.ca**) has various online bulletins, one of which is entitled "Cross-Border TaxBreaks."

General Tips

Almost all tax-related Web sites have something to offer by way of free tax tips. But KPMG has outdone itself by offering a "Tax Tips of the Day" mailing list (to subscribe, send an e-mail to **majordomo@kpmg.ca** with the text "subscribe taxtips"). It covers a multitude of detailed tax topics. It may not be the most entertaining read, but the information is current, and can save you some tax dollars.

Newsgroups are everywhere, and the tax area is no exception. By participating (either by browsing or by posting, too) in newsgroups such as **can.taxes**, you can get a feel for what the "hot" tax topics are and what people are doing to reduce their taxes.

Some pretty creative (and perfectly legal) ideas often come from here! But don't jump on just any advice you hear! That's because the name of the tax "game" is avoidance, not evasion. Some newsgroups, unfortunately, may contain material that veers towards the latter!

Direct Advice

Speaking of advice, you can access a plethora of tax advisors (and tax return preparation services) who advertise on the Web as a first step to getting your business. Sympatico's Maple Square directory (**maplesquare.sympatico.ca**) is a uniquely Canadian repository of links to various Web sites. Click on "Business and Economy," followed by "Taxes." There, you can access tax practitioner information, such as services offered and type of advice provided. But heed my earlier recommendations—online "advice" can be fraught with risk if you're not careful!

Time to File

Now that you've obtained the tax forms, educated yourself about tax rules, and sought online or personal advice, you're ready to file your return. But do you file it yourself or hand this task over to your tax practitioner? This is a personal decision based mainly on the complexity of your financial situation and how proficient you are with tax rules. Remember: the larger the tax practice, the larger the fees usually are. You should only get the tax services you really need. Don't get sold on services you don't require. By learning tax basics through the Net, you're in a better position to avoid this trap!

If you go the "do-it-yourself" route, you still have more choices. You can prepare the tax return manually or can use tax preparation software. If you choose the latter route, the two best-known products are QuickTax and CanTax. Both offer online support, free revisions or corrections, and other information to help you along. Their respective sites are **www.intuit.com/canada/ quicktax** and **www.cantax.com**. In addition to the technical side of things, these sites also provide useful tax tips.

Finally, while it is still not possible to actually file a tax return to RevCan online (unless you yourself are an authorized E-file tax preparer), you can use the Internet as a conduit to do this. For example, INTERtax (**foxall.com/intertax**) allows you to e-mail your basic tax information through online forms. Foxall Income Tax Services compiles and processes your personal tax information and e-mails duly completed forms to you. All you do after that is print out copies and send them to RevCan. The cost of their service is comparable to the fees charged by other tax return preparation companies.

Insurance

As a Canadian over fifty, there are many reasons why you should consider your current and future life insurance needs. Some of these reasons will become evident in the discussion that follows. And there are just as many types of policies available as there are insurance needs. There are policies for your home, posses-sions, automobile, health, life, business interruption, and travel, to name just a few. What does each particular policy do? Why do you need it? When, given your age, is the best time to buy it? Where and how do you purchase it? Any one of these questions can trigger hours of tedious research—unless of course you take at face value what is communicated to you by your insurance representative!

Once again, and as you will see throughout this book, this is where the Net comes in as a valuable information-gathering tool. With it, you can address all of the above issues and more. The

Net's online resources will educate you before you have to reach an insurance-related decision. Do you have more coverage than you need? Do you need more coverage? Do you understand insurance basics? Questions such as these can be efficiently answered or addressed with the Internet. Here's how.

Let's Go to Insurance School

Proper research of insurance products is the first step to addressing "insurance need" issues. I say this for a number of reasons, not the least of which include the need to overcome:

- complex policies and terminology,
- confusion over multiple options,
- salesperson pressure, and
- the lack of comparative information.

Once these obstacles are overcome, you can better address the issue of your need for insurance.

The benefit of the Internet here is that as a tool, it strikes a balance between knowing too little about insurance and knowing too much. You're not trying to become an insurance agent, but you don't want to be exposed to unnecessary costs either!

Research starts with understanding. You've got to "learn the lingo" if you're going to browse insurance Web sites! A good place to do this is with the Merritt Insurance Glossary at **www.insweb.com/entry/insurance.htm**. Here, you will learn the nuances between "term" and "whole life" insurance. You can also browse their FAQs, facts and statistics, and online articles. Another site that discusses similar topics can be found with the Insurance News Network at **www.insure.com/**. It's strong on links to insurance-related sites.

You'll also want to know about the Canadian Insurance industry. You'll want a national "big picture." A quick browse through Insurance Canada's pages (**www.insurance-canada.ca/insurcan**) will give you a "feel" for domestic insurance industry issues. You can access consumer information, a useful insurance provider directory, and related Web sites. A similar resource is provided by the Insurance Bureau of Canada (**www.ibc.ca**). Here you can access consumer-oriented information such as home and auto insurance primers, safety tips, and locations of insurance organizations.

Also note that many of the insurance company sites discussed in this section of the chapter also have Web pages that provide primers on various insurance topics.

Insurance—Choices, Choices

Now that you understand the terminology, you're in a better position to deal with the different types of insurance policies that exist. Here's a rundown on the most popular types of policies available.

Debt and Taxes

Insurance companies are now providing life insurance more readily to those over fifty. As a mature Canadian, you need to ask yourself whether life insurance at your stage in life will

- cover your funeral costs,
- allow you to pay off your debts (and/or taxes) at death, and
- leave you enough money to bequest to your spouse and children (estate planning).

Buying too much or too little life insurance can both be costly mistakes—you'll need information.

To access this information, you will be steered towards several on-line indices of relevant providers (brokers and insurance companies) of insurance. Most of these providers have insurance products geared to retirees and near-retirees. While it is not possible to list all of these carriers here, I have provided the URLs to some sites that do attempt to list most carriers.

Here's to Your Health!

Mature Canadians are statistically more prone to illness than others. This is a fact of life. You'll therefore want to make sure that you're covered for medical emergencies that may arise from time to time. What if you don't have an employer-sponsored plan? What if your provincial health plan doesn't cover certain costs? For many over fifty, these are unfortunate realities. How much does health-related coverage cost? And what's the difference between disability, dismemberment, medical, and hybrid health-related policies? Often, these questions remain to be answered.

Specifically, many mature individuals have to cope with disabling conditions such as arthritis or other physical conditions that affect mobility. Although you cannot know for sure what the future holds for you health-wise, your personal preferences or circumstances may spark an interest in disability insurance. If so, answers to key questions about disability insurance can be found at Insurance Inlinea (**www.inlinea.com**). Click on the "Disability" page link for related information. Inlinea's Web pages, touted as being "consumer-oriented sources of insurance information," provide not only disability insurance information, but also allow you to get quotes. Here, you can even get advice on life and term annuities, automobile insurance, and health insurance (such as what key provisions to look for). You can also access practical life insurance and estate planning tips.

Travelling Around

Mature Canadians love to travel. With the children grown up and with perhaps a little more disposable income on hand, travel becomes more of an option. It doesn't matter whether you take a trip up north or across the world—you'll likely want travel insurance.

If you're travelling out of the province or country, your first stop should be at your provincial Health Ministry Web site. (Their Web addresses are listed in the last section of this chapter or can be accessed through **canada.gc.ca/othergov/prov_e.html**.) There, you can find out what your regular provincial government out-of-province health coverage is. You can also read up on special rules regarding how travel-related health services are paid for, and how much the dollar coverage is. You need to know what these rules are. Why? Because it's the basis of knowing whether you will need more insurance—private travel insurance to be exact! More on where to find such private-sector providers later. Because governments frequently modify many programs as part of their budget cutting process, and because the Net is a great way to get current, up-to-date information, this strategy only makes sense. Of course, you can also place a phone call. But all bets are that you'll have a long wait before you get a live person—also popular budget cut targets! Besides, such information, often complex, is best obtained in "print."

Home Sweet Home

Many mature Canadians depend on the equity built up in their homes, considering them to be a retirement nest egg. If you're a property owner, you want to make sure that a disaster won't wipe out many years of savings.

One of the better home insurance resources belongs to General Accident Insurance (**www.genacc.ca**). Here you can obtain a wide range of online home-related and general insurance advice. Through the useful hotlinks provided, you can access local insurance broker and association sites, and safety and crime prevention advice.

As for keeping your doors locked and being safe, browse the Insurance Information Institute's site at **www.iii.org/consumer.htm**, where you can get tips on home safety, reducing insurance costs, and filing claims.

From Lemon to Limousine

Mature Canadians love to drive. This is the primary means by which they get to work, or to play! But do you really need that high-premium-attracting, low deductible for your clunker? By contrast, did you really get the best quote and coverage for your expensive Caddy?

Again, the General Accident Insurance and Insurance Information Institute Web sites will hold some answers for you, as will many other sites discussed in this section.

Now That I Know About Insurance, Where Can I Get It?

The choices as to what policies you need can be overwhelming; the cost downright frightening! You now know a little more about insurance, and the types of policies that exist; but you may still be asking yourself—what do I do next?

One mistake frequently made by Canadians is that they do not price the same type of policy with different carriers (or different financial institutions). CIBC, for example, is a bank that offers insurance. Likewise, some insurance companies act more like banks. Things gets more mixed up all the time!

Another option you need to know about (or likely already do) is that insurance can be purchased through an organization directly or through an agent or broker working on behalf of several insurance companies or banks. What are the differences? Which is best for you? One of the better Web resources to help you address these questions was created by the Independent Insurance

Agents of America (**www.northwesternmutual.com**). Their FAQ list is strong and their advice often applies to Canadian insurance consumers.

My recommendation is that as long as you have done some advance research on what policies are available, why you need them, and where you can get them, your final decision can be based on price and quality of service. Before the Internet's resources were available, you were comparing apples with oranges. With its resources at your fingertips, you can now compare apples and apples—a much better foundation on which to base a decision!

Directories

In Part I of this book, I discussed the usefulness of Internet directories. The biggest is Yahoo. Browse through their listing of Canadian insurance carriers and brokers at **www.yahoo.com/ Business_and_Economy/Companies/Financial_Services/Insurance/ Regional/Countries/Canada**. Click on the relevant area-specific Web link to narrow down your search to a more local level. There you will find references to Web page after Web page of insurance providers—pages that in most cases also have useful information about insurance. As these pages evolve in complexity, interactivity, and security, you will also notice that over time, more and more will start to provide online quotes and comparative prices. This is an advantage that you can claim for yourself.

Special Insurance Considerations for Those over Fifty

If you're part of a company plan now, but see yourself retiring soon, consider an arrangement with your employer to continue your policy after your retirement. You may have to continue paying your share as well as your former employer's share of premiums, but the combined premiums may still be a lot less than those for individual plans.

After you've maximized the coverage you can get from your employer, consider augmenting it with private insurance. This is a good idea for many persons over fifty since the older you get, the harder it will become to get cheaper (or any) coverage later. Once you pass the physical, make sure that the policy cannot be cancelled by the insurer due to subsequent changes to your health. Having done so, you will have peace of mind that your estate concerns are taken care of.

Although U.S. in focus, the Senior Resource site (**www.seniorresource.com/insur.htm**) contains tips on long-term care insurance, and provides links to related seniors' Web resources. It too is a developing site.

And don't forget Fifty-Plus.Net (**www.fifty-plus.net**). This is a storehouse of product and service discounts—many insurance-related—for Canadians over fifty. From the Fifty-Plus.Net home page, click on "The Learning Centre" to find out more about discounted insurance products.

Too Much, Too Little Insurance

Now that you know what type of insurance you require and where you can get it, you still need to determine how much actual coverage you will need. Again, your selection of company or agent will be the principle factor behind this decision. The quality of their advice to you will weigh heavily on what policy and how much coverage you will buy. So how can the Internet help you here?

To get second opinions of sorts, check out "tip" pages such as the Insurance Information Institute's "Ways to Lower Your Insurance Costs" (**www.iii.org/consumer.htm**), offering cost saving tips on everything from health insurance to car insurance.

Also, many of the companies listed in Yahoo's directory will also provide helpful, unbiased cost-saving and other tips on their Web pages. A small investment in "Web time" may save you some money—at the touch of a button!

Finally, to get an excellent overview of all insurance issues, Jim Carroll and Rick Broadhead's *Canadian Money Management Online* (Prentice Hall) is, in my opinion, a great source of this type of information.

Managing Your Retirement Online

As a Canadian over fifty, you have probably been inundated with ads telling you how to plan for your retirement. For this stage of life, the term "planning" is a misnomer because it ignores, for the most part, what Canadians can do now to improve their quality of life. "Planning," as it applies to older Canadians, is an overused and marketing-oriented buzz word that seeks to trap all people in one net.

The concept of "retirement management" (RM) was something that I introduced in my first book, *Ontario Retirement Handbook*. It represents a different response and approach to dealing with key issues of concern to mature Canadians.

What Is Retirement Management?

Under RM, retirement issues are not defined as being only financial matters and only planning actions. Instead, health, housing, and leisure-related issues are also addressed. These three lifestyle issues (the way you approach non-financial issues and free time) ultimately impact on finances anyway. They also impact your overall quality of life (the quality achieved when one re-source, say investment, is traded off for another, say travel). Quality of life is a personal choice, not one that can be dictated by a financial planner that may turn a blind eye to your less tangible needs.

Retirement management also recognizes that retirees need to know what they can do now regarding financial and non-financial (lifestyle) issues. Prime examples of this are government programs (discussed in the next section). Many retirees and near-retirees over fifty are missing out on the many federal, provincial, and municipal programs and services that exist just for them because they are unaware of them. Financial planners can't charge you for this information, so they usually don't tell you about it! The politicians are also "bottom-line" oriented. At election time, they often fail to adequately address seniors' programs or programs for "older" (45+) taxpayers. After they're elected, however, such programs usually become targets of clawbacks and curtailments. Witness the last federal election and the "stands" on seniors' programs of all parties. Precisely—there were no "stands!"

Retirement management is also intended to apply to all income groups. You'd think by reading the ads that if you don't have more than $100 000 in your bank account, your business is not wanted. In fact, some financial planners have actually placed (and advertised) client net worth limits! This is insulting. Finally, RM seeks to reveal and address the many still-valuable public-sector options; and does likewise for private-sector options.

These are the fundamental principles of retirement management. Whenever you are confronted with a retirement-related decision, base it on a retirement management approach. In other words, know the "big picture" of retirement.

Why Is Retirement Management Important?

Although the components of RM (finances, housing, health, leisure, etc.) all form separate chapters in this book, it is important to view them in holistic terms. One component can't be addressed without affecting the other. Therefore, you need to understand these relationships. You need to understand RM.

Role of the Internet in Retirement Management

What about the Internet? What is its role in retirement management? Simply stated, retirement resources on the Net arm you with information that helps you make sound retirement decisions. But you say, "Books do that!" True. But books cost money and Net information is usually free. Furthermore, some of the RM-related information on the Net is only available on the Net! Print versions of online RM-related resources seldom exist, or are difficult to find at best. Nevertheless, you should approach the Net as a supplementary source of retirement management information.

While Internet-delivered resources on RM are few and far between, two insightful and creative Web sites have emerged—perhaps the only two you really need—that have captured the essence of the retirement management concept. The first is RetireWeb (**www.retireweb.com**), a Canadian provider of "quantitative and referral-oriented retirement information." The second, an especially powerful RM site, is that of MetLife (**www.metlife. com**), a U.S insurer that has many "advice and fact-oriented" resources for your stage of life. Together, they strike a perfect balance in providing what you need to know about RM. Even so, be advised that Metlife's information is of U.S. origin and is not a complete substitute for similar advice from a qualified professional.

The Metlife Life Events Line

MetLife's Web site (**www.metlife.com/Lifeadvi/advice.html**) covers all sorts of fifty-plus topics. Just look at the illustration below and you will see the very broad range of financial and nonfinancial topics covered. At least thirty of the topics illustrated directly apply to the current or potential needs of those over fifty. Many of these Life Events Line pages represent a good, one-stop source of common-sense, "fifty-plus" advice that MetLife calls "Life Advice." Retired or not, these online advice pages likely have something for you. And even though the topics have insurance sales "hooks," the core advice is useful nonetheless.

A Quick Example

By starting at the Metlife home page, you will see that you can find a Life Advice topic by going to their Life Events Line and clicking a topic that interests you. Alternately, you can use the built-in search tool. Try adding the word "retirement" into their "About

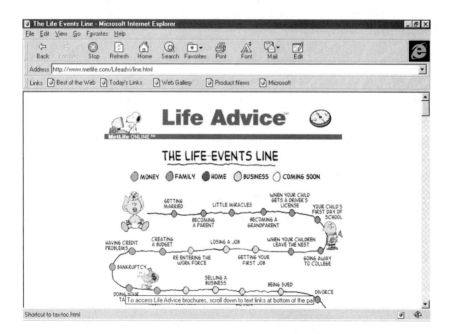

Money" search engine. I did. I found over 40 relevant topics that linked to even more relevant information!

RetireWeb

This site (www.retireweb.com) is not as comprehensive as that of MetLife, but considering the fact that it was designed by one individual, it's almost as impressive!

RetireWeb is strong on the "number crunching" side of things and is full of information and utilities to help you manage your finances as you move toward retirement. If you're already into retirement, it has information specific to your age bracket. One example of a utility that is useful for all age groups is the assortment of cash flow calculators available online. These will tell you how much you have to save now in order to get "X" amount of dollars in the future. (This is not a surprising feature since a qualified actuary, Scott Parkinson, designed this Web site.) One of the more nerve-rattling features of this Web site is the life expectancy predictor. You anonymously enter in your vital statistics and out comes your age of death! Of course, this is based on actuarial experience and is probably not far off from what you would have guessed anyway. But it's fun. I think.

In addition to the calculators (which quite effectively replace the need for complex and expensive software), you have Web advice that is geared to different stages of life (pre-, post-, and at-retirement). The pages are not as comprehensive as the calculator pages, but over time, I'm confident that their content will expand.

Finally, there's the "Other Internet Sites" page at **www.retireweb. com/othersites.html** that makes up for MetLife's lack of "purely Canadian" content. Here, links are provided to some of the best financial and non-financial Web sites in the retirement and financial fields. Not surprisingly, Gordon Pape's and CARP's sites are included among these links!

Government Financial Resources Online

I believe that news of the imminent fall of social programs for seniors is largely exaggerated. Firstly, it's not based on fact. Of the recent federal and provincial program cuts, few of the major cuts affected seniors. While there will be constant adjustment to many programs—such as CPP and OAS (adjustments such as tougher clawbacks, lower benefits, higher contribution rates, new Seniors Benefit, etc.), I doubt that any will be replaced or cancelled outright, even some of the smaller programs. This is because politicians know how to use calculators well. They know the demographics. As Canada ages, voters will not tolerate drastic seniors' program cuts. Even some boomers who may feel that seniors "have had it easy" in Canada will lose this argument. Why? Politicians who cut seniors programs do so at their own peril. However, a positive outcome of this battle for scarce public resources will be that seniors programs will become more and more needs-based. They'll be fairer. Politics, like accounting, remains a numbers game.

Internet and Government

You'll know what I mean when I tell you that it's a hassle to find out (through printed material and phone calls) what government programs are out there. If you're lucky enough to find out about them, the information is either too sketchy, too detailed, or too complex. When you try to pull it all together, it gets even more difficult. Add in the federal, provincial, and municipal providers of these programs and you're looking at a one-week-long information-gathering exercise. Also, because programs change so rapidly, half of what you compiled is probably out of date. It won't be printed again until next year and you certainly wouldn't look forward to going through the labyrinth of government voice mail again. Get the picture?

The Canadian government actually has a good history with the Internet. Would you be surprised if I told you that in many cases, government has outperformed the private-sector in providing creative, unbiased, and useful Web sites? Governments, along with individuals, represent the original driving forces behind the Net. It is only after business recognized the commercial potential of the Internet that business took over as the new impetus behind it.

Government Programs and Services

The Internet is an efficient and effective way to link you to government program and service information. The major programs for older Canadians, otherwise known as entitlements, are delivered at the federal level. Many other important ones are delivered at a more regional or local level. Before continuing further, it's a good idea to take a look at some of these major programs.

The Human Resources Development Canada (HRDC) "Programs and Services" page at **www.hrdc-drhc.gc.ca/hrdc/proind_e.html** contains a large selection of information about income security and other programs. There is even an "Older Canadians" link (**www.hrdc-drhc.gc.ca/hrdc/dept/facts/intro_e.html**), which points mature Canadians to information they need to know.

Old Age Security (OAS)

OAS is paid to about 3.6 million Canadians aged 65 and over. Everyone over 65 is eligible, but the OAS you receive is subject to clawback. This in turn triggers tax planning opportunities. (Recall that tax issues and related Internet resources were discussed previously in this chapter.)

The HRDC Web site (**www.hrdc-drhc.gc.ca.hrdc/isp/oas/ oasind_e.html**) has all the OAS information you need, and provides Web site referrals and office locations too. Current payment rates are provided on a timely basis, keeping you up-to-date of changes at the click of a mouse button.

Guaranteed Income Supplement (GIS)
This is an additional entitlement conferred to those seniors receiving full or partial OAS and who have little or no additional income. Web information at HRDC includes eligibility requirements, benefit levels and important deadlines. Fully eight percent of GIS recipients miss annual renewal deadlines. Reading through the HRDC site may provide you with a useful reminder of these deadlines.

The Seniors Benefit
Introduced in a federal budget, the Senior's Benefit proposes to replace the OAS, GIS, pension income credit, and the age credit in 2001. Seniors who were 60 or older at the end of 1995 and their spouses (regardless of age) have an option of either getting benefits under the new system or receiving benefits under the existing OAS/GIS system for the rest of their lives. Those who were not 60 at the end of 1995 automatically fall under Seniors Benefit proposals.

What exactly are these proposals? Confusion over this area abounds, as does controversy. The Seniors Benefit is heralded by government as a fair system (it claws back more for higher income earners). At the same time it is criticized by wealthier retirees and near retirees as a disincentive to save for retirement (saving more means losing more). The Internet takes you to this debate and discussion. Enter "senior's benefit" into your favourite search engine and a list of current articles will appear.

Because of even more recently-announced clawbacks, and because a decision has to be made by the year 2001, tax planning is called for. The KPMG and Ernst & Young accounting sites (discussed previously in this chapter) provide useful discussion and tips.

Spouse' Allowance and Widowed Spouse's Allowance (SPA/WSPA)

SPA is a monthly federal allowance for seniors between 60 and 64 whose spouse is over 64 and receiving OAS and the GIS. It is not taxable. The rules for WSPA are almost identical to those of SPA. Additional information can be accessed through the "Older Canadians" HRDC link at **www.hrdc-drhc.gc.ca/hrdc/dept/ facts/intro_e.html.**

Canada Pension Plan

For CPP information, go to **www.hrdc-drhc.gc.ca/hrdc/isp/ cpp/cppind_e.html.** The Web pages are numerous owing to the complexity of this entitlement and the need to break it down into more understandable components. The topics below speak to this.

Overview
Retirement Pension
Disability Benefits
Survivor Benefits
Credit Splitting
FAQs
Current CPP Rates
News Releases

The Internet is a great way to get CPP-related information. The facts are current, quickly accessible, and come right from the source program. Many a time have I been confounded by newspaper articles that were either inaccurate or only provided one piece to a much larger and more complicated puzzle. The HRDC site is a one-stop, accurate, and current resource. The HRDC news releases are also invaluable and more detailed than the bulletins received along with your CPP payment. And if you want even more detailed CPP information, go to the Canada Pension Plan Consultations page at **www.cpp.rpc.gc.ca/homepage.htm**.

A good summary of most federal programs and the proposed Seniors Benefit Program can also be found at RetireWeb (**www. retireweb.com/finance/govtprograms.html**). A master list of all federal programs, agencies, and departments can be accessed at **canada.gc.ca/depts/major/depind_e.html**. You should know this site well—it's a handy Web index for many "fifty-plus" issues we'll be seeing throughout this book.

Provincial and Municipal Programs

The following are examples of entitlements and programs commonly delivered at the provincial, city, and municipal levels:

• Family Benefits Assistance
• Income Supplements
• Older Worker Adjustment Programs
• Senior's Property Tax Credits
• Senior's Sales Tax Credits
• Tax Exemptions and Grants for Home Adaptations
• Veteran's Assistance
• Welfare Assistance

To find out how your province, city, or municipality delivers these programs, you'll need to go to their home page and work your way through their indices. The resources are too numerous to list here and doing so would not provide you with any added value. It's an efficient search approach that counts. Use a search engine with the above-noted terms as key words to find this information. Many provincial Web sites also have their own built-in search tools and links to other government Web sites. The following table lists provincial home pages.

Provincial and Territorial Home Pages	
Provincial government home pages can be found at www.gov. followed by:	
Alberta	**ab.ca** (i.e. www.gov.ab.ca)
British Columbia	**bc.ca**
Manitoba	**mb.ca**
New Brunswick	**nb.ca**
Newfoundland	**nf.ca**
Nova Scotia	**ns.ca**
Ontario	**on.ca**
Prince Edward Island	**pe.ca**
Saskatchewan	**sk.ca**
Quebec	**www.gouv.qc.ca**
Northwest Territories	**www.gov.nt.ca**

The Web sites noted in the table above can be used as handy reference sources for many of your government program information needs. They will be referred to throughout this book.

Chapter 5

Back to Work and Down to Business

In this chapter, discussion will focus on one of the most important 50+ issues of the day—the ability of mature Canadians to generate extra income through employment or business means. The issues presented next are relevant to anyone over fifty—regardless of the level of need for extra income. This is because decisions about getting "back to work" or "down to business" are not always driven by financial need. Sometimes, it's a question of personal preference.

There's nothing like a statistical overview to help you gauge where you stand within your peer group. The table below portrays a compelling retirement landscape for all working or non-working Canadians.

Employment and Business Facts

About 250 000 Canadians between 50–64 will be unemployed in 1997.[1]

Key obstacles to re-employment or getting into business were age discrimination, lack of education and training for older workers, and out-of-date skills.[1, 2]

Employer bias is a very significant barrier to employment for older job seekers.[2]

Barriers to re-employment appear to reside more in the environment in which employment is sought than in personal characteristics.[2]

Someone 50 and unemployed will face the same employment barriers as someone 62 and out of work.[2]

The number of retirees under age 60 in the 1990s is double that of two decades ago, and the median retirement age in 1997 was 62.[3]

The percentage of Canadians retiring before age 60 in the 1990s is currently 34 percent.[3]

From 1984 to 1995, the segment of the Canadian labour force comprised of 50+ workers increased by 14%. During the same period, the labour force of 40 to 50 year olds ballooned by 60%. This trailing workforce (i.e., your competition) is growing.[1]

Almost 50% of Canadians that retired (voluntarily or not) before 65 years of age would have otherwise remained in the workforce.[1]

Almost 25% of North American retirees hold jobs—about half for the financial rewards, and the other half for the personal satisfaction and fulfillment. About one third of the 35 million American Association of Retired Person (CARP's U.S. counterpart) members work in some capacity and another third state that they would like to be working.[4]

Many seniors' groups agree that there is a growing trend for persons over fifty to seek to go back to work or be in business for themselves. Whether they return to work because they need to or want to generate extra income is still under debate. Another issue is whether they are physically-able to return to work.

For those thinking about getting back into the workforce or into business, the common reasons cited were the need or perceived need for structure, social interaction, status, identity, and control. And of course, there was the ever-growing financial reason.[4]

The country that can harness the talents of its older population will have the competitive edge economically.[2]

(1) Twombly, Dianne. Getting Back to Work. Toronto, Canada: Macmillan 1997.
(2) One Voice, "Options 45+" Report and Survey 1997.
(3) Statistics Canada, "Perspectives on Labour and Income" Journal 1997.
(4) American Association of Retired Persons, Washington, D.C.

As you can see from these facts, the need or desire to generate extra income doesn't seem to end at 65 after all! And employment options abound too. For example, many mature Canadians use retirement as a launching pad into a new, more satisfying career. Others choose to be entrepreneurs and launch their own businesses, capitalizing on their years of experience. And others who are already retired for some time choose to try to re-enter the business fray. The key word here is try, and for good reason. There are obstacles faced by older workers or retirees that don't exist for their younger counterparts. Both the employment and business-related sections of this chapter will deal with these obstacles. An Internet-based approach to help you re-enter the workforce or business world will be presented. However, to apply Internet resources properly, you first need to know the key issues and you need some preliminary advice to get you started.

Employment

The 50+ Employment Landscape

To fully understand the "fifty-plus" Canadian employment landscape, you need to recognize why barriers for older workers exist and what your true employment needs really are.

Why Are Older Workers Being Forced Out of the Workforce?

Aside from the fact that the Canadian population is aging, the labour market itself is changing. This market is trying to cope with the introduction of technology, globalization of competition, and organizational and economic uncertainty. It is ironic that the first two forces, technology and globalization, are the essential ingredients of the Internet—the very tool that can help you get back on track. Whether this track leads you to another job or to entrepreneurship, the Internet is a powerful tool that can help you reach either objective.

Your Employment Objectives

As a job seeker, you may find yourself in one of several situations. You may be working now, but wish to make a late career change. You may have been forced from work involuntarily, but need or wish to get back to work, regardless of the type of career. You may have retired already, but find yourself wanting to fill free time with traditional work. These are just some of the employment situations you may be in.

Regardless of circumstance, you should start planning your response in advance. This applies whether you are still employed, are looking at other work options, or are considering entrepreneurial or hybrid choices. As part of this planning process, key issues to be addressed include the following:

- What are your needs and personal preferences?
- What is your health status?
- Are you going to need employment income or do you prefer to fill some of your free time with work?
- Will you keep your current job or get a new job?
- If you seek a new job, are you actually ready and trained for the new position?
- Do you prefer emotional reward over financial reward?
- Will earning income cause your government entitlements to be clawed back significantly?

- When you do finally retire, are your health and mobility going to be acceptable enough to let you enjoy this period?

To help you reach a sound decision, reflect on these issues carefully. Discuss them with your financial advisor. Talk things over with your spouse and with friends. They may give you new insights. Many of the Web advisory sites to be mentioned in this chapter can provide you with help in this particular area.

Overcoming the Obstacles to Employment

Aside from the obstacles and issues cited in the list above, other issues facing older workers include chronic unemployment, physical impediments, government program cutbacks, increasing life expectancies, and new family pressures such as those faced by workers who must also be spousal caregivers. Corporate mergers, downsizing, closures, and restructuring—the buzzwords of today—make an already difficult situation even worse.

Traditional job search strategies need to be modified to suit the needs of those over fifty. The good news is that these strategies can now incorporate the many job-search resources available through the Internet. Using the Net as a tool, various resources are revealed that can put you at an advantage—even over younger competitors. It is critical to be familiar with these resources. Without them, it's definitely more of an uphill struggle.

Before looking at these resources in detail, it is necessary to review three basic principles for a 50+ job search:

- Know employer misconceptions and hurdles
- Know yourself
- Use the Internet's resources to put you at an advantage

Know the Misconceptions and Hurdles

Familiarity with employer-imposed roadblocks is a key step to effectively overcome ageism—society's collection of misconceptions about older workers. What are these misconceptions? A prospective employer may believe that older employees:

- Resist change
- Take more time off
- Already have a lot of money and don't really need more
- Expect more salary dollars than others
- Do not or cannot work as hard as others
- Don't want to work for a younger boss
- Can't learn new things quickly and efficiently

With all of these misconceptions, it's no wonder that many older workers get discouraged from re-entering the labour force. My advice? There is no need for overreaction or despair. Instead, take some pro-active steps to help your situation! Your response? Make sure that your résumé and interview is sensitive to and addresses these issues! More on this later.

Know Yourself

Knowledge of your goals, skills, strengths, and limitations will help you arrive at a realistic job search plan. Weighing these issues against your values and interests will help you reach an honest self-assessment.

Start by taking stock of your skills, abilities, and accomplishments. Employers seek thinking skills, a sense of responsibility, positive outlook, receptiveness to change and teamwork, and good communication skills. Older workers must ensure that they have most of these. If not, they must develop them through training or general change of attitude.

If you have a degree, diploma, or certificate, you have proven yourself to be a thinker. If you have work experience, you have likewise proven yourself as a thinker. The point I'm trying to make is that you should not underestimate your talent simply because you've been out of the educational system or out of the workforce for a while. Highlight your accomplishments; and always remain confident.

Use the Internet's Resources to Put You at an Advantage

The Internet resources to be presented in this chapter are important to know about. In fact, 85% of Canada Employment Centre counsellors who responded to a survey entitled "Options 45+" agreed that "older workers were unaware of services available to them." The Internet helps reveal these services.

But as with any tool, you first need to know why you should use it and when it is appropriate. The need for a good Internet-based job search approach is reinforced by the fact that over 87% of Options 45+ survey respondents also said that "older workers lacked advanced job search skills." This chapter will shed some light on how you can acquire or strengthen your existing job search skills.

Employment Options

Whether you're still working or looking for work, there are more employment-related options than you probably realized. Most of these are discussed next.

Stay Where You Are!

If you're still working now, the best move to make may very well be no move at all. If you're comfortable with your current job, thoroughly fulfilled, and not anxious to leave, you should probably stay. However, there may be a catch. Keeping your current job is often a challenge, especially in these cost-cutting times. More and more organizations are offering early retirement packages. In some cases, "offering" represents generous terminology. In other cases, an early retirement package may be too good to refuse. No matter how much you may want to stay, the choice may not seem to be yours to make. Or is it?

Compromise on Hours Consider arranging a part-time, temporary, or flexible work schedule with your company. This way you are still working, but you've gained some leisure time too. And many companies have set up programs to accommodate their retiring employees. Find out more about your employer's retirement policies and see how well the policy fits into your financial and retirement objectives.

Consult for Your Company (or Its Customers!) Like temporary or casual work, you can work as a consultant on a *perdiem* or fixed-fee basis for your company. You'll be able to use your current skill set and avoid immediate re-training by staying in the same line of work.

You may also want to consider consulting for other companies in your field. These may include suppliers or customers currently doing business with your employer. When the time is right, throw these ideas "up in the air" to everyone concerned. Explain that you offer relevant experience and a different perspective on industry, business, or technical matters. The best "employment" options are often the less obvious ones such as these!

A Totally New Job or Career

Whether you're working or out of work, choosing a new job or career is a complex decision—one that ultimately has to be made by you. Finding a new job in your previous industry is hard enough. But if you're considering an altogether brand-new career, you need to address some additional issues. What new vocation really interests you? Do your current skills match your new interest? Does this new career require lots of re-training?

This is just a sampling of issues that need to be addressed. Internet resources abound to help you answer these questions, whether it's a new job or a new career you're after.

Your New Career Short List—Research It! Research the jobs and careers that interest you to enable you to make a good "new career" decision. This is where the Internet comes in handy. I will shortly outline some of the more job- and career-specific Internet resources that will undoubtedly be of help to you in this area.

Effective job research should start out with basic "offline" approaches such as going to the library and reading up on the different careers you're considering. Check out the trade and professional publications for a particular industry. Read up on different companies. Get a university or college course calendar to get an idea of training time and cost. Flip through the yellow pages to see if you can come across an occupation that pops out at you and looks appealing. Even call your local chamber of commerce to find out about their job-related services.

Human Resource Development Canada (HRDC) Government, despite the popular perception that it's a technological laggard, has actually done quite well in terms of establishing relevant, useful, and up-to-date Web resources. Information on government-sponsored programs and services abounds, and career programs and services are no exception. One of your first stops should be Human Resource Development Canada's (HRDC's) Web site at **www.hrdc-drhc.gc.ca**. Their many pages and indices explain or address various topics including:

- Labour-related resources (**labour-travail.hrdc-drhc.gc.ca/eng**)
- Income security programs (such as Employment Insurance)
- Other programs (such as Canada Educational Loans Program and Program for Older Worker Adjustment)
- FAQs
- Social security reform

HRDC also has an extensive library whose collections, many job related, are catalogued online by subject. The library can be accessed at **www.hrdc-drhc.gc.ca/hrdc/library/libe.html**. Click on the PRIMO Online Catalogue icon to access HRDC's library database. Through PRIMO, look for any publications, reports, or articles related to job search strategies, career choices, or descriptions of trades and professions.

HRDC's Job Search page (**www.hrdc-drhc.gc.ca/hrdc/job/jobind_e.html**) has a series of "new career" resources. Also, the World of Work Directory, another resource, can help you locate information on almost anything related to employment. Career Development is a link that will help you in the area of skills development. Finally, the Electronic Labour Exchange can be perused for local jobs—it's an online job bulletin board!

Finally, Human Resource Centres (**www.hrdc-drhc.gc.ca/maps/national/canada.shtml**) can help you in many career researching areas. The centres are located across the country and this Web page links you to them. It's a good way of finding out about their locations, hours, and types of services they can provide.

Provincial Government Job Resources Because many job-training programs are delivered at the provincial level, you should always visit your provincial government's home page for information on skills development. This material will put a more local spin on your research and will inform you about the existence of any special programs geared to training older workers. Click your way around their departmental or Ministry pages until you find the Ministry of Labour, Ministry of Education, or a skills development-related agency. Again provincial government home pages can be found at **www.gov.** followed by **ab.ca** (Alberta), **bc.ca** (British Columbia), **mb.ca** (Manitoba), **nb.ca** (New Brunswick), **nf.ca** (Newfoundland), **ns.ca** (Nova Scotia), **on.ca** (Ontario), **pe.ca** (Prince Edward Island), **sk.ca** (Saskatchewan). For Quebec and the Northwest Territories, the respective Web addresses are **www.gouv.qc.ca** and **www.gov.nt.ca**.

Other Organizations Options 45+ is a joint initiative undertaken by the Federal government and One Voice—a seniors' advisory group. It aims to promote the value of older workers to Canadian employers. The Options 45+ home page (**www.mbnet.mb.ca/scip/options45%2b/**) lets you access publications, newsgroups, and employment resources (**www.mbnet.mb.ca/scip/options45%2b/inet.html**) specifically geared to mature workers. Their links are highly relevant to any "fifty-plus" job-related issue.

CanWorkNet (**www.canworknet.ca/user/sitemap.html**) is a directory that is oriented towards the job or career "planning" side of things. CanWorkNet can help you with career and job search planning, provide you with job market information, provide advice if you have a disability or special need, and refer you to online material on just about anything to do with finding a job or new career. This site also lets you search online employment resources by subject or location.

A wealth of other new job and career-related information is available online. Using your browser, type into the subject search field the name of the trade or occupation that interests you. But be aware that you may come up with "hits" (leads to web sites fulfilling your search criteria) from around the world. Also, while this type of hit-or-miss approach can be fruitful, it can likewise be time consuming if you've found too many resources.

Again, don't forget the traditional approach. Talk to someone that's already in the trade or profession. Arrange to meet. Come prepared, respecting the fact that this individual has taken time to see you. Being brief and forthright will yield you great first-hand information about your career of interest!

Exactly How Much Work Can You Do? Your Other Options
Whether you wish to stay with your current employer (assuming you're still employed now), or seek totally different employ-

ment, there are other options to consider, all with their own sets of issues. Some of these options are listed below.

Other Employment Options
(With a Current or New Employer)

Arrange flexible working arrangements (flex time)
Work for less pay or seek a less intense job
Work part-time
Work as a temporary or casual employee
Work on call or on contract

All of these options provide you with the potential to spend less time or energy at work. Are any of these choices right for you? Predictably, these alternatives should appeal to you if:

- You're a professional who still wants to "keep your hand in."
- You enjoy personal contact with others, and want to preserve this opportunity.
- You enjoy your leisure time, but need just a little more income to sustain your desired lifestyle.

Preparation for a New Job Search

Online and On-site Learning

Upgrading your skills through continuing education is the next step to take once you've decided on a career or job change. Going to an interview armed with a certificate or diploma will put you at a distinct advantage—or at least remove another job change obstacle. Your willingness to learn new things speaks volumes about your commitment to better yourself. Combined with your experience, your new skill set may very well put you ahead of other competitors.

When should you upgrade? Essentially, any time you want to make yourself more marketable or anytime you want to change your line of work. Sometimes, technological change will outright force you to update your skills.

How does the Internet fit in? Open a newspaper today and you will likely see ads from schools offering online courses in various cities, either through closed-circuit TV or on the Net. These courses are full credit, bona fide sessions designed to help you reach your educational goals. You can apply to attend online, or attend traditional, in-house courses as a mature student. The best way to get information is to access college and university Web sites. Look for course calendars, fees, and eligibility criteria on these pages. It's a lot faster than a series of phone calls or personal visits.

Despite the fact that many mature Canadians are willing to retrain themselves, misconceptions and ageism still persist. What can you do about it? For starters, maintain a positive outlook based on the fact that many recruiters are beginning to realize that academic background is no equivalent for actual work experience, something that you likely possess in abundance. At every opportunity, highlight your dependability (older workers take fewer sick days than their younger counterparts) and stability (older workers are less inclined than a younger person to suddenly leave a company).

Know the Employment "Rules" and Resources

Age doesn't change the basic steps that constitute job hunting. *Get Wired, You're Hired*, by Mark Swartz (Prentice Hall Canada), is a very helpful "rulebook" resource for this aspect of your job search. It describes in great detail how you can use the Internet to help you in your search. This is especially valuable if mobility is a concern for you.

Before submitting your résumé, first talk to some friends and colleagues. Try to get leads from them. Such referrals are valuable.

And don't be timid, remembering to talk to anyone that may be able to help you. Put your pride aside!

The Fifty-Plus Résumé

A critical step in preparing for your job search is the way you will communicate what you have to offer. To this effect, you'll need an up-to-date résumé. And for anyone over 50, I recommend a "combination" résumé format, rather than a "chronological" format. While a chronological format, where you list employment experience in reverse chronological order, is most common, this format draws too much attention to dates. Instead, use a combination style, in which you first organize your résumé with skill headings. Then, list your job titles, places of employment, and dates at the end. This format plays up your skills and you can emphasize specific accomplishments.

Some additional résumé tips are presented below. While these tips will not apply to all situations, they offer general guidance that you should consider in earnest.

Ten Tips for a 50+ Résumé

Keep the résumé short (no more than two pages) and use bullet form.

Keep the résumé clean, avoiding stains, handwritten corrections, and fancy paper.

Exclude personal data such as age or religion.

Use numbers in your résumé since helpful statistics stand out and highlight the point.

Remember to include your address and telephone number.

Minimise your educational background—unless education is critical to getting the position. Your key contributions to a prospective employer at this stage in your life are your skills and experiences.

If you've only ever worked for one employer, place more emphasis on your skills, accomplishments, and your last position.

If you were a homemaker, include this in your résumé. Tease the marketable skills out of what you did at home. The book *What Color is Your Parachute: The Net Guide* by Richard Bolles (Ten Speed Press) may help in this regard.

Eliminate early employment or other information that has no bearing on your prospective employer's current requirements.

Be specific in your descriptions. Don't rely on generalizations and flippant phrases. Being older means you have expertise on your side—let it come across in your résumé. Cite concrete examples and specific accomplishments.

An online resource that can help you construct a résumé is Career Marketing—Résumé Services at **www.careermarketing.com**. It's a résumé preparation service that also provides newsletter advice on the basics of résumé preparation.

Another good résumé-related resource is CareerCity (**www.careercity.com**), where you can acquire résumé advice and take advantage of a résumé posting service. While it's predominantly a U.S. site, the résumé-related advice is useful to everyone, including Canadians.

Internet Job Search Strategies

Network With Others

The Internet is a superior networking tool. But before we get to the tools of networking, let's review some of its principles.

Simply stated, networking is the deliberate and sometimes scripted interaction with others to help you meet your personal objective(s). These persons may include friends, family, alumni, club members, former co-workers, or just about anyone else for that matter. Networking is something that you must do. If you're already a pro at it, great! If not, learn it. It is commonly said that it is not what you know, but who you know that is the key to finding a job!

When networking, communicate three things:

1. Your objective,
2. Your skills and talents, and
3. Exactly how the other person you are networking with can help you with (1).

Networking, to be effective, should be followed-up with subsequent contact, and should always be done in a tactful, respectful, and natural manner.

The Internet is ideally suited to networking. One job-specific resource that is available to mature job seekers is the Canadian Network for Experienced Workers (**www.mbnet.mb.ca/scip/ options45%2b**). This Options 45+ site has an established, electronic network that links mature workers with companies, employment agencies, and government programs and services.

It doesn't stop there. One Voice, one of the sponsors of the Options 45+ site, has also developed seminars and presentations aimed at publicizing mature workers to employers and other organizations. It has created training programs and produced literature—all designed to provide support to older workers across Canada.

Tour the Internet

Aside from actively networking, you can also "browse" job listings on the Internet. This is somewhat more of a passive approach. Nonetheless, it's something you also have to do. *The Canada Employment Weekly* (CEW) (**www.mediacorp2.com**) is

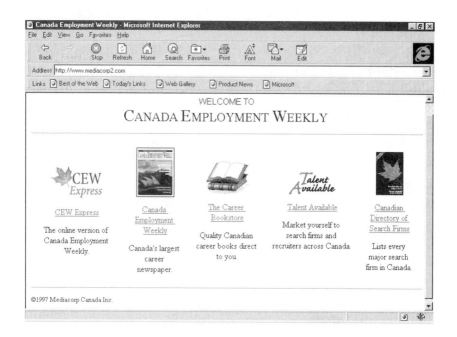

a popular Canadian career newspaper for persons in all stages of life. *CEW Express*, the online version of CEW, lets you access their job-related ads and feature articles. In addition, the CEW Web site itself provides job-related tips, links you to their career bookstore, and provides a directory of search firms.

A good employment-related site to visit is The Riley Guide (**www.dbm.com/jobguide/internet.html**). Here, you can locate many job-related resources and access local Freenets and bulletin boards.

CareerMosaic Canada (**canada.careermosaic.com**) is a good site to access some of the top employers (and jobs) in Canada and abroad. Features include a jobs database, career resource centre, online job fairs, and an employer directory. This site allows you to search job listings using keywords as well as geographic location. You can even enter your résumé into CareerMosaic's résumé service.

CareerMosaic's main Net competitor is E-Span (**www.espan.com**), which also allows for flexible online searches and résumé downloads into a database. Career Internetworking (**www.careerkey.com**) has online job postings, provides general employment-related tips, and also allows you to list yourself as a job seeker. Its search tool accommodates geographic, industry, or vocation-based searches.

More job listing and matching services are provided in appendix I. Although they are geared to all age groups, everyone over fifty should know about them. Finally, remember to use your search engine and newsreader. They are useful job-search tools. Although they can present you with information overload, they can be extremely handy if you're looking for a very specific vocation or opportunity but don't know where to turn. For Web sites, enter the name of your trade or profession into your search engine. For newsgroups, run through the hierarchy of **can.jobs** until you find a sub-category that meets your needs. Or, post your own message of availability. Don't worry—for job-related postings you won't get flamed.

You've Landed the Interview

Mirror, Mirror

There are just three things to remember—prepare, prepare, and prepare. Research the company. If the organization that's granting you an interview is publicly traded or is a large private company, its background can likely be found on the Internet. Or, visit an investment Web site such as **www.techstocks.com**. Here, like at the other investment sites I discussed earlier in this book, you can find corporate background information such as recent press releases and annual report extracts. As for current activities, over 50 000 news and press releases can be accessed at Newswire (**www.newswire.ca**). Having this knowledge cannot help but impress your interviewer.

Next, ensure that you make the right physical impression from the very start. This means good appearance, body language, and attitude. Look the part of a successful, polished professional. Don't give the interviewer any reason to think of you as being old. More and more people are taking the grey out of their hair, losing weight, and shaving off their beards—all to help project a younger image. While it's important to "be yourself", such grooming has to be weighed against your need for a job and the prejudices that exist out there. Don't forget to look the interviewer in the eye. Smile often and maintain a confident stance. Speak in a commanding but not overbearing voice. Believe in yourself, keep yourself psyched up, and don't apologize for anything, especially your age.

Finally, sell the interviewer with your conversation. Point out that you possess the right background and experience for the job. Advertise specific accomplishments. Emphasize age-related advantages—you have no young children and possess lots of experience. Never discuss age-related physical impediments and never give out your age.

Let some time pass after the interview. Then, follow-up with a friendly and business-like phone call. With this approach, and a little luck, you may be back to work!

Entrepreneurship

You may have been retired for some time now. Or you may have only left the workforce recently, voluntarily or not. For every person that seeks to re-enter the workforce as an employee under these circumstances, there is another who wishes to finally start the business they've dreamed of—to be an entrepreneur.

In North America, there are over 47 million full- or part-time home businesses. And according to Statistics Canada, 825 000 people were self-employed. Both numbers are growing steadily. Why? As you have probably heard all too often, companies and governments continue to cut back staff. They prefer contract work, with the resultant lower benefit payments and higher flexibility. Cost cutting and staff reduction is the executive's mantra. Few get to retire at 65! Technology also continues to displace workers, pushing early retirement thresholds to even lower ages, as Statistics Canada has recently revealed.

But many have found that the "fifty-plus" stage of life represents an ideal time to strike out on their own. After all, companies are looking for businesses to service their needs, more so than individuals *per se*. They want your talent and wealth of experience, but packaged under a business name. They seek to minimize their "employee benefit" and "union" quandaries, even if the business they contract work to has just one employee—you!

No longer confined to a company rule book, many retirees and near-retirees are tempted to take the plunge and start something they can call all their own. Entrepreneurial success, however, requires the addressing of two fundamental issues:

- What you need to know before starting a business—careful planning
- What you need to do after starting a business—Internet networking

If you're considering entrepreneurship, the Internet can serve you well on both counts.

Advance Business Planning and Research

Terrance Berscheid of Vancouver Island, British Columbia (berscht@pinc.com) shares how the Internet has helped him start a business after he "retired."

Having retired from the (Canadian) Coast Guard at the young age of 50, I was worried that I'd have to give up my Internet "social-net". Now, one year later, I am using the Internet more than ever to keep in contact with my former colleagues. I also started up my own training business, and communicate and teach through the Internet. It's a very efficient productivity tool for educators.

Terrance Berscheid also cited Strategis (**strategis.ic.gc.ca**, discussed later in this chapter), as one of the Internet resources that helped him launch his business. The Internet allowed him to reach out and network with others—for work and for keeping in touch with friends.

Is Entrepreneurship Right for You?

For anyone at the "fifty-plus" stage of life, personal and physical limitations must be addressed before embarking on an entrepreneurial route. And spousal commitments cannot be ignored. You have to ask yourself "Is this option right for me?"

For mature Canadians, the traditional self-employment "suitability checklists" found in many small business books need to be re-evaluated. Many of these generic lists fail to address concerns of older businesspeople. Consider the issues below.

The Fifty-Plus Small Business Self-Assessment

Are you physically able to spend long hours nurturing your business? Is your health conducive to entrepreneurship?

What do your spouse or other family members think of your desire to be a 50+ entrepreneur? Are they fully aware of the dollar- and time-related sacrifice that is required? Are you aware?

Will you be comfortable with a possible lack of stability at this stage in life?

Are you willing to spend large amounts of retirement-time working without guarantee of future income?

Are you willing to risk financial loss? If so, can your retirement finances absorb such losses?

Have you ever worked in a business similar to the one you're considering starting?

Have you worked for yourself before?

Do you possess sufficient business skills and experience?

Are you decisive?

Do you generate good ideas, and possess initiative and commitment?

Are you confident, positive, creative, energetic, self-motivated, and calm?

Do you possess time-management skills?

The Ins and Outs of Entrepreneurship

Read All About It There are various books out there dealing with starting-up a small business. The last time I was at The World's Biggest Bookstore in Toronto, I was amazed to see literally hundreds of different books about starting up a small- or home-based business! But if you want to zero-in on a book that is specialized, perhaps a book dealing strictly with the "personal" aspects of running a "training" business, check out the offerings of the online bookseller Amazon.com at **www.amazon.com**.

Amazon.com is a distributor of tens of thousands of books. This Internet-based resource is especially handy if you don't live near a large bookstore or library but still need good, current information. Their collection of small business publications probably includes exactly what you need—specific help addressing many small business issues. If the issues listed in the table above haven't scared you away yet, then you may very well be ready for the next step—thoroughly researching your business area.

Business Development Bank of Canada (BDB) If there's one small-business site that has it all, it's here at BDB (**www.bdc.ca**), where you can get lots of business planning and related information. At BDB's site, you can get information on financing, managing, starting-up, and marketing a business. For example, the BDB has the "Step Up" program for women entrepreneurs. It also provides term loans for qualified businesses. However, the most powerful feature of this site is its outright comprehensive set of links to other small business Web sites. Click on "Web Resources" and you will be provided with a list of Web resources under the headings of "Start-Up," "Business Planning," "Research," and "Government."

One particularly useful link is to the online version of HRDC's "Minding Your Own Business" publication. It's written in a straightforward way and the coverage of key issues is very good. You can read about business planning, review the pros and cons of home businesses, and can take a "small business test" to see if entrepreneurship is right for you.

Other Business Planning Resources From the TD Bank's home page at **www.tdbank.ca** (or through BDB's Web links), you can access and participate in an online small business forum, moderated by Larry Easto—small-business expert and author of *How to Succeed In Your Own Business* (available for free at most TD branches). In this forum, you can post questions and read Easto's comments.

The Royal Bank (**www.royalbank.com/english/bus/bigidea**) lets you access "The Big Idea For Small Business", a Web site containing many recommendations on how to plan and start a business, and provides an overview of small businesses in Canada.

It also includes an interactive software program designed to help you create a business plan. Many consultants charge for this service. Here, you can develop a reasonable business plan for free.

The Virtual Business Link (**www.cbsc.org/alberta/main.html**) has a solid collection of online publications in their "Virtual Library." There, you can download publications on small business planning, market research, and other business start-up materials. It also has good links to other Web sites and has referrals to government programs (for example Reference Canada).

The ever-present Microsoft, not to be outdone anywhere or by anyone, has a good site at **www.microsoft.com/canada/smallbiz**. Here, you can get home business tax planning tips, review a bibliography of business books, link to other Web sites, and read up on the success stories of others.

With all of the resources mentioned above, trust me, you don't need more! But if you are looking for something really specific, try Yahoo Canada (**www.yahoo.ca**). Once there, enter key words such as "entrepreneurship" or "home business." Or, click on "Business and Economy," followed by "Small Business Information" and "Directories."

Next Step: In-depth Research

Why research deeply into business issues? Haven't you done enough already? Research is critical because you will invariably have to face a truly startling statistic—more than half of all small businesses fail within five years of their start-up. Why do these small businesses fail at such a dismal rate? Almost always, failure arose from lack of preparedness—or lack of planning.

Business planning involves research. And research should include accessing Internet resources. The Internet is simply too powerful a tool to ignore in business planning.

In addition to researching the materials within the Web resources already presented, two additional areas needing to be researched are:

Business financing issues
Marketing issues

Researching Financial Issues Financial issues are so critical that you should consider all of the points in the Financial Requirements checklist below. Remember, lack of funds is a key reason for small business failures.

Financial Requirements Checklist

How much money do you need initially? How much money can you put in?
Do you have enough money to keep the business afloat for at least one year?
Do you know how much credit you can get from suppliers?
What net cash flow (income) can you expect from the business?
Can you financially manage to put all or some of your salary or income back into the business?

Take a close look at these issues and make sure that you have addressed them properly. Failing to do so can result in disaster. You'll also need help along the way. This includes professional help—something I always recommend. Professionals such as accountants, lawyers, and business advisors can help you get off the ground and keep you going. But the Web can provide you with initial small business financing information too.

The Bank of Montreal recently introduced a new Small Business

Loans program. This program can loan you start-up capital. You can start off at their site map on their home page at **www.bmo.com**. From there, click on "Small Business Rates and Products" to get more specifics in areas such as preferred rates and business services. Web links to other financing-oriented sites are also provided, except those of competitors, of course! But don't forget the other banks—financing is their business.

Preparing to Sell Your Mousetrap What business should you start? What product or service should you sell? These are some of the issues of marketing.

Choosing the type of business that's best for you is probably the most complex issue. Both personal factors (listed previously) and environmental factors come into play. Some of the environmental factors include the current national and local business and industry climate. Part of the business start-up decision also involves deciding on whether you want to run a "goods" enterprise (commonly referred to as retailing or manufacturing) or "services" enterprise. The pros and cons of each are discussed in many of the Web resources presented already—so I won't repeat what you can find elsewhere.

If you've decided on the way you want to do business and are thinking of buying an existing one, the Regional Business Opportunities "InBusiness Canada" site (**www.rbo.com**) gives you a good sense of the variety of businesses out there. There, you can browse a database of businesses for sale, franchise opportunities, and related material. And the information is free.

You can also visit the realty sites discussed in chapter 7. The same real estate resources that can help you with housing decisions can do likewise with your business purchase decision. Finally, consider the following home office/self-employment issues.

Pros and Cons of Home Offices/Self-employment

Pros

Incur lower initial capital and ongoing operating costs

Avoid excessive commuting

Do it your way with your ideas

Obtain more personal satisfaction, freedom, and rewards

Take advantage of tax write-offs (see the section on finance-taxes)

Work flexible hours

Cons

Will be disrupting family routine with business

May find that space is at a premium; and persons over fifty will face ergonomic issues (such as proper seating, lighting, and mobility)

May get distracted by TV or food

Will be at beck and call of customers

May feel isolated

Franchises

Franchising is one business structure that is very popular amongst those over fifty. Essentially a "turnkey" business, the franchisee requires a relatively smaller investment. As a franchisee, you have the benefit of dealing with a bigger company, which can offer you some guidance, marketing networks, and an established brand name.

In brief, when you enter into a franchising contract, you make a capital investment in the franchise, agree to operate your franchise according to the conditions set by the franchisor, and agree to buy all your products from the franchiser. In return, the franchiser helps out with financing, promotion, bookkeeping, management, and training. These are big benefits if you have never run a business before. In essence, you are buying "experience."

However, be aware of the drawbacks to franchising. Franchise frauds and poor business practices are on the rise—so be careful in your research. Many of the business planning resources discussed previously include ample information on franchises. An additional resource can be found at Be the Boss (**www.betheboss.com**). Here, the nuts and bolts of franchising are explained in a straightforward manner.

Getting the Word Out

If you want to advertise your home business on the Web, read *The Canadian Internet Advantage* (Prentice Hall) by Jim Carroll and Rick Broadhead. It's the definitive Canadian publication that takes you through the five W's of setting up your own Web site. It also provides many wise caveats to those entrepreneurs wishing to explore this route. Another book with similar themes is Mary Cronin's *Doing Business on the Internet* (Van Nostrand Reinhold). It is more a "why-to" rather than a "how-to" book, thus complementing Carroll and Broadhead's book very well.

And don't forget the old-fashioned way of promoting your business. Personal referrals continue to be valuable, yet have nothing to do with the Internet. The best way to get such referrals is to never forget the personal touch to business—ever! Stay in touch (at least by phone) with customers and clients. Join clubs and do presentations. These can include speeches, seminars, or workshops. Write proposals, publish brochures, engage in advertising, send out direct mail, and take advantage of any free public relations opportunity (such as announcing your new business in your local community newspaper).

Where Are Your Customers?

In a sense, everywhere—including the Internet! One of the best ways to network for the mature Canadian entrepreneur is through Internet! Why? For two basic reasons. First, your mobility may not be what it used to be. The second reason is that the Internet in Canada is growing at a steady rate. In 1998, over 1.4 million households (over 12 %) will have access to the Net. By the year 2000, this figure (according to Corinfo Research and Information Inc.) is expected to jump to 2.6 million households (almost 25%).

The Net places you on a more level playing field with the larger companies, especially if your products or services are specialized.

Starting the Business: Internet Networking

What You Need to Do

Now that you've spent some time planning and researching, are you ready to actually start a business? If so, the Internet has additional resources with exactly the type of help you will need.

Strategis Industry Canada's "Strategis" site (**strategis.ic.gc.ca**) claims to be "Canada's largest online collection of small business information." You can access business information by sector, business support services, regulations governing business, training programs, and statistics. These topics represent ongoing information requirements once you're up and running.

In addition, directories are provided for relevant government agencies and loan providers. Strategis also has excellent content in terms of how the Internet can be introduced into your marketing plan even after your business has already started up. This site has hyper-links to a storehouse of additional information about running a business. It also has a search tool organized by industry sector. With this information, you can better respond to market developments. Overviews of franchises, advertising services, and networking resources are also available here. This site is very complete.

Other Business Operation Resources Industry Canada and the provinces jointly fund the 12 Canadian Business Service Centers (CBSC), whose Web site is at **cbsc.org**. These centres are geared to those businesspeople interested in obtaining special publications and online access to other information such as overviews of federal and provincial government business programs. The CBSC site also allows you to access a database of statistical and business information. If mobility is a problem for you, then this resource can be invaluable.

The Export Development Corporation of Canada (**www.edc.ca**) has a wealth of FAQs, small business information, useful hotlinks, and, if you're really thinking big, domestic and international market information.

The Self-Employment Assistance Program (**www.the-wire.com/ sedi/seanet.html**) is targeted to persons receiving Employment Insurance payments and who require training to help them start and run an ongoing business. Like Strategis, it's government program-oriented. And don't forget the provincial Ministries dealing with industry, trade, and economic development. They are generally good, up-to-date sites specializing in local business issues. Their offerings are similar to those of the Federal government.

The Most Boring Part of It All—Record Keeping

Actually, record-keeping is not as bad as it used to be, what with all of the accounting software available to be run on your PC (or downloaded for those on network PCs). The large accounting firm sites, identified in the taxes section of chapter 4, are ideal for quick, free financial reporting advice. Just don't hire them as your accountants! This is because while they are competent, they're also relatively expensive if all you are doing is setting up a small business! Instead, I would recommend that you use a professional accounting practitioner or even a qualified bookkeeper to start.

It Starts to Add up

Most new entrepreneurs are taken aback by the amount of time it takes to physically set up a new business. It takes even more—time and money—to keep it running smoothly! So don't forget that ongoing businesses require ongoing expenditures! Expenses include bank charges (credit card, line of credit, current account), government registrations and declarations, insurance (maintaining the adequacy of the existing policy, determining the need for liability or business interruption coverage), PC hardware and software (choosing among new offerings, allocating the cost and time to learn), and office equipment and supplies.

Old Fashioned Tips—A Last Word

There's lots of "business tip" information on the Net. Too much. It can confuse, confound, and overwhelm. So I just wanted to leave you with some fundamentals. Keep steady hours—not too much, not too little. Have a separate business phone line. Follow your business plan, whether you have changed it or not. Minimize your chance of getting distracted from business. Sub-contract some of your work if you've got too much. If you have a service business, do one project at a time, especially if they are big and have deadlines. Finally, if you have a home office, keep your office away from your family area. I believe that these basic "personal welfare" tips will help you stay on top of things, and allow you to enjoy your near-retirement years to their fullest.

Chapter 6

Health Care on the Net

As someone over fifty, a natural extension of the aging process means that health-care issues gain importance to you. It is also important to recognize that the maintenance of your good health, or a speedy recovery from ill-health, is based on two things happening: access to information about health-care and access to health-care itself.

For most of us, a trip to the doctor means a fairly long wait just to get into the examination room, followed by what is often a rushed checkup. What with all of the government cutbacks—rightly or wrongly—and other health-care controversies, is it really surprising that both doctor and patient come out of the whole experience a little more stressed? Would it be fair to assume that a system that could only devote a series of brief examinations to an Alzheimer or stroke patient is only partially effective? Would it not also make sense to get better information if you could?

Because of the wealth of medical information available on the Internet, doctors now share information that used to reside, for the most part, in their exclusive domain. Now that the public can share in this information, the patient is in a better position to become a good consumer of health-care information.

While the Internet cannot, and should not, replace a visit to your doctor (after all, a physical examination is the prerequisite to, and basis of, proper treatment), its resources can assist you in accessing quick, useful, and current information. You can obtain information and advice on your current symptoms, find out about alternative treatments, get second opinions, and access advice on staying healthy. Many health-related Web sites serve to help you form questions in preparation for your next doctor's visit. The information will also increase your knowledge of your own body—the end result being a better chance at even healthier living!

This chapter will help you learn how to wield some very special tools of the Internet—current, flexible, and powerful health-related resources that will help you overcome or mitigate the common difficulties of getting to a doctor and obtaining sufficient medical advice. You will also learn that avoiding the quacks, and there are many, involves due diligence. And because health issues (other than how a government provides the programs) are mostly universal, the Canadian, U.S., and some international sites presented next are all useful.

This chapter has been organized to resemble how medical information is found on the Internet. It will show you how you can access online medical encyclopaedias, Web sites specializing in certain medical conditions, online health magazines and journals, electronic drug references, and resources devoted to alternative health-care. Other Internet health-care resources are organized along professional lines and include nurses, pharmacists, dieticians, psychologists, and dentists. These sites are also pointed out and discussed. And although I have already stressed that online advice can never replace physical examination (that is, personal access to care), online resources do exist to help you get actual advice—that is, a doctor's "digital diagnosis!"

Next follow some of the most comprehensive and reliable health-care resources on the Internet. Other sites not mentioned here are presented in the appendix. Still others not mentioned in this book can be found through an organized approach as outlined in the next section.

Finally, keep in mind that some of the newest medical treatment information will likely find itself seeded in the Internet before anywhere else. Timely and organized information can make all the difference if you're suffering from a certain ailment.

Searching for Online Health Resources

You can search for health-related Internet resources in one or both of the following ways:

By individual medical topics or professions
By type of information

Search by Topic

Using a Search Tool

Topical keyword searches can be done through search tools or directories (discussed in chapter 2). The table below lists some of the many terms that you can include as a search engine keyword.

Browser Keywords

(For Effective Health-Care Resource Searches)

alternative health	health care	pharmacy
chiropody	medical	pharmaceutical
chiropractic	medicine	psychology
dental	nutrition	physiotherapy

| diet | ophthalmology | specific names of illnesses |
| health | optometry | specific names of associations or professions |

Using a Directory

If you seek a comprehensive directory of medical topics, the Medical Matrix (**www.medmatrix.org/index.asp**) is one stop that will make your search more effective. This site contains comprehensive links to online resources categorized by medical condition. Conditions listed include those that persons over fifty are especially at risk of encountering. Medical Matrix also categorizes its index by medical literature and professional occupation. Its links are ranked and reviewed, a critical Web feature any time something as important as your health is at stake. Here, you can also access discussion forums, educational, and pharmaceutical resources.

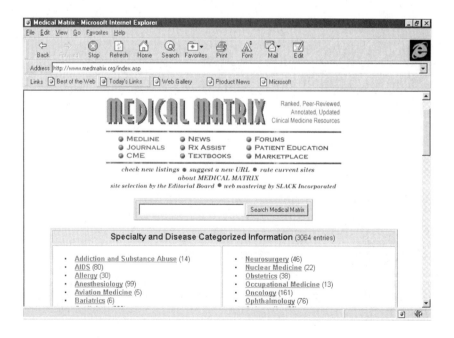

The Internet has a wide variety of searchable online medical information presented at various levels of sophistication. Research materials, consumer health information, periodicals, and articles form the foundation of online health-information. The Web, newsgroup, and other Internet tools and resources are the way to get at them!

Before continuing on, you may want to get a feel for the types of resources that will be discussed in this chapter. If so, jump right into the following leading medical sites. They can be found through the following conduits:

Internet Resources

World Wide Web

Sympatico	**www1.sympatico.ca/** **healthyway/health2.html**
Yahoo	**www.yahoo.com/Health**
Medical Matrix	**www.medmatrix.org**
Health on the Net	**www.hon.ch**

Commercial Services

America Online (AOL)	Keyword **HEALTH**
Compuserve	Go **HEALTH**
Microsoft Network (MSN)	Go **HEALTH**

When the commercial services started out with just their own content (that is, no Internet access), one thing that they did well from the start was form a good online health database. Now that they provide both content and Internet access, they still have this original health-related content. Although this book does not focus on commercial ISPs (because not everyone with Internet access has access to commercial service content), the four preceding sites merited acknowledgement.

Search by Type of Information

In a search by topic, you already have an idea about what to search for. In a search by type of information, you now need to figure out where to search. Why? Because some information (such as recent medical breakthroughs) is more conducive to, say, journal formats than other information (such as first aid). Being an efficient "searcher" of the Net means that you should possess an organized and logical approach. The table below lists the types of medical information available and where you can access these resources.

Types of Medical Information

Type	Location
General reference material	Topical health Web sites (via Yahoo)
Magazine and news articles	Your Health Daily (**nytsyn.com/live/Lead**) Other sites (via InfoSeek)
Journal articles	Medweb (**www.gen.emory.edu/medweb**)
Illustrations and graphics	Topical health and medical school Web sites (via AltaVista, MetaCrawler, and InfoSeek)
Education, tips, and referrals	Association and government Web sites (via Yahoo)
Discussion forums	Newsgroup FAQs and mailing lists (via DejaNews)

When browsing a medical Web site, quality of content is critical. (For guidance on identifying quality Web sites, refer to the checklist found in the "Managing Your Investments on the Web" section of chapter 4. Although geared to investment Web pages, the principles embodied in this checklist are general enough to also apply to many other categories of Web resources.)

General Online Health Encyclopaedias

Although some of the more age-associated conditions experienced by those over fifty—arthritis, menopause, Alzheimer's, and cancer—are specific areas of interest and have associated Web sites, it's always a good idea to first become familiar with the more general Internet resources available. Online health encyclopaedias (OHEs)—whose home pages are essentially tables of contents—represent logical starting points for most general health information searches. Often sponsored by established and respected organizations, these sites have a higher level of credibility than their less structured counterparts. They focus on building their own content, and generally steer away from too many links.

One of the better online health encyclopaedias is Med Help International (**medhlp.netusa.net/index.htm**). Here, you can get plain language medical information about many illnesses. With its large main online publications library and its specialized statistical database, Med Help is very comprehensive. Despite its abundance of scientific medical content, the facts are usually presented in layperson's terms.

Healthtouch Online (**www.healthtouch.com**), another OHE, has a directory for "older persons." Topics covered here include most of the conditions commonly encountered by older men and women. Most of the online resources are well referenced so you know where the information is coming from. You can search Healthtouch with its keyword search tool or use one of its drug or medical information sub-directories.

Medical Online (**www.medicalonline.com.au**) is another site that has comprehensive, proprietary content. (Again, this is unlike many health-care Web sites that only provide links to other Web sites.) It's the closest thing to the full online encyclopaedias typically found in many commercial ISPs.

The Harvard Medical Gopher (**gopher://gopher.med.harvard. edu**)—gives you access to its library's online catalogue and other medical publications. Need I say more?

MedAccess (**www.medaccess.com/first_aid/fa_toc.htm**) is a comprehensive site for almost any "health and wellness" information requirement. There is a seniors' resource page at (**www1. medaccess.com/seniors/senior_toc.htm**), where you can access relevant online publications, food guides, physical and mental well-being tips, and many other guides and resources for seniors.

If you need referrals to more information, the Medical Information Resource Centre's site can point you in the right direction. It's found at **emporium.turnpike.net**. Click on "health and medicine" and this site will provide you with comprehensive lists of health topics and referrals to other online resources. While it's essentially a link-oriented jump station, the sites referred to tend to be the more credible ones.

If you still can't find what you're looking for, or if you're prepared to pay a fee for even more detailed medical information, you may want to consider online databases maintained by larger companies. One of the biggest and most popular is Medline, a medical resource that is used by many medical professionals. By going to the Medical Matrix page discussed earlier—**www.medmatrix.org**—you can access both free as well as pay-as-you-go information services such as Medline. Although complex in terminology, they may suit your information needs.

Specialized Online Health Resources

The only thing that mattered to Glenna Pike, retired widow and grandmother to seven pre-schoolers, was her grandchildren! Their welfare was her passion—and health was at the very top of that list. As an "online grandmother," she used the Net to full advantage in this regard. Here's how.

> *Health-related (specialized) Internet sites were a logical starting point for me. Actually, I use the information more for my children's (and their kids') benefit than even myself! From the newsgroups, I was able to get an assortment of pretty good advice on colic—something that my son's child was going through. I downloaded a list of colic tips from the **misc.health** and **alt.support** discussion groups. I stay away from any site or resource that recommends eating or drinking anything that's not considered to be a common food or beverage. Drugs are totally out of the question! It's funny how my sons seem to take my advice more seriously when I tell them it came from the Internet! One of my sons finally opted for my (a discussion group's) tip of running a cool mist humidifier in a far corner of the baby's room. Apparently, the noise seemed to soothe the child to sleep and my son got a decent night's sleep!*

Pike's personal account contained one critical piece of advice that can't be stressed enough—her implicit advice about avoiding online tips from someone "playing doctor." A lot of discussion groups are rife with bad information. Pike used the online resources properly. She first obtained relevant information and then sifted through it with a critical eye.

My advice is to approach online health-care resources with a combination of scepticism and willingness to try something new but safe. Use your common sense. Evaluate the source of the information by digging deeper into source material and the studies referred to. Knowing this, let's now turn our sights to some specific resources.

Arthritis

This disease can affect everyone; but no one more so than a person over fifty. In this country, Arthritis Canada (**www.arthritis.ca**) represents a key online resource for information about this disease. Their site has information about coping with arthritis and shows you where to access related provincial programs. It also has a simple but effective set of links to similar sites.

You can get even more information about arthritis at The U.S. Arthritis Foundation (**www.arthritis.org**). Many pages of useful facts, tips, and resources are presented.

If you wish to search a newsgroup for discussion and support, you need not look any further than **alt.support.arthritis** and **misc.health.arthritis**.

Let's pause here for a moment. Having scanned these arthritis-related newsgroups, you may have already learned two quick lessons. The first lesson, touched on in Part I, is that you could add just about any extension to a newsgroup address such as **misc.health** to find discussion on a particular health-related topic. This is important to know when searching for health resources. For example, you could replace the extension arthritis (**misc.health.arthritis**) with the extension cancer (**misc.health.cancer**).

The second and more important lesson is that because many of these newsgroups are unmoderated (unscreened), you're exposed to a plethora of—forgive the politically insensitive cliche—"old wives' tales." While it is not my intention to pass judgement on the quality of "advice" given by discussion group contributors, I believe that extra caution is called for when it comes to health-related advice. I was shocked to see an arthritis posting that advocated cod liver oil because it "oils your joints!" Perhaps this posting would have found a better home in the **alt.comedy** newsgroup!

Alzheimer's Disease

Statistics Canada reported that the number of seniors suffering from Alzheimer's disease and other forms of "dementia" will triple over the next 35 years. In other words, close to 800 000 Canadian seniors will suffer some form of dementia by the year 2032. Alzheimer's will affect two thirds of this total. More than half of the 250 000 Canadians currently suffering from dementia live in long-term care facilities. The economic and personal costs are enormous, and government cannot be expected to buffer this problem in its entirety. All seniors need to explore their options here. In other words, know your housing, health-care, and personal options. The Net can present these to you.

The Alzheimer Disease Research Centre (ADRC) Web site at the University of Washington (**www.biostat.wustl.edu/alzheimer**) is both comprehensive and credible. Through these Web pages, you'll be able to access the research centre's online archives. These archives include literature and recommendations on symptoms, current treatments, and other information. Discussion threads (trails of dialogue) are also accessible. Nursing home issues are adeptly dealt with at this site.

The Alzheimer's Disease Web Page (**med-amsa.bu.edu/Alzheimer**) is also a resourceful and informative Web site to visit. It is especially strong on family issues and caregiver options. It's a good complement to the ADRC site.

If you choose the newsgroup route for accessing Alzheimer's information, such as with an **alt.support.alzheimers** discussion group, remember that you can opt to include your e-mail address in the posting to allow others to reply to you personally. Since this is a very active site, be prepared to be inundated with reply e-mails!

Menopause

Did you know that menopause represents a multi-million-dollar health-care sub-industry? Every day, more than 4 000 North American women of various ages enter this stage of life; books, articles, and other sources of information abound—and the Internet is no exception to this growth phenomenon!

This area is one that invites lots of alternative medical advice. Just search the Web with the keywords "alternative health-care," "herbs," and "naturopathy and menopause," and you'll see what I mean—lots of menopause-related sites. When searching for these keywords, you'll also likely come across a page called Menopause Matters (**world.std.com/~susan207**), which emphasizes herbal treatment. It's ample extra reading for those undergoing menopause and who still crave more information.

The newsgroups are, as always, a good place to visit for support. This is because you'll get a good sense of what the issues are and how others are coping with this condition. The **alt.support. menopause** discussion group seems to have had fewer of the offbeat pieces of "advice" than those found in the arthritis newsgroup. I say this because the advice in the former group was more frequently supported by references to medical periodicals and comprehensive bibliographies. A good sign!

Alcoholism

Many persons over fifty have to (or know someone who has to) deal with this problem. It's not surprising in a way—many of life's greater pressures coalesce at this stage in life. Deaths, family displacement, termination of career, and other major life adjustments often seem to happen at once. For many, alcohol becomes a viable coping "solution" when in reality, it's a grave problem. But one is wise to act quickly. The older a person gets, the more of a drain (financial and emotional) the battle against it becomes. The Internet, once again, can lend support in this area as well.

Of all group support therapies, the 12-Step Alcoholics Anonymous (AA) method is perhaps the most well-known. It is based on group interaction, monitoring, and support. The Internet, while not as personal as face-to-face interaction, nevertheless makes the recovery process easier—a dimension that is a critical first step on the road to recovery.

One of the first things one needs to do is to get informed about the nuts and bolts of the alcoholism recovery process. One Web site that promotes the formal 12-step AA recovery method can be found at **www.recovery.org/aa**. It's a good, easy-to-read (non-technical) site that lets persons access AA-related online literature and conference information, and also provides you with access to E-zines on the topic.

A second thing you need to consider involves the AA centrepiece of recovery—group therapy. The Internet is very much about groups, especially when you utilize the third Internet "pillar"— newsgroups. Potential alcoholism-related newsgroup stopovers include **alt.psychology.help**, **alt.psychology.personality**, and **alt. support.depression**. When you scan the threads (links) of postings, you'll be reading some pretty bleak material. But the persons getting this problem out in the open are the very same ones most likely to succeed in recovery. They are to be commended!

Heart Disease

The Heart (**sln2.fi.edu/biosci/heart.html**) is a Web site that shows you how to prevent and cope with heart disease. If this is a condition you face, this site provides tips on how to monitor your cardiological fitness. You can even take a test to see where you stand in relation to healthy peers! The Heart also takes you through the process of how this vital organ actually works. It does so with good graphics—and the downloading time is reasonable. Its many resources include extensive links to related sites and referrals to support groups.

In Canada, about 80 000 persons die annually from cardiovascular disease. In fact, as the many statistics found in the Canadian Heart and Stroke Foundation's Web site (**www.hsf.ca**) bear out, the risks increase dramatically with age. But this site provides you with a response—an education and preventative-care-based response. It has links to provincial Foundations and many related topical sites as well. Its statistical database is both extensive and sobering. This site also deals with the next topic—stroke.

Stroke

There are an estimated 250 000 to 300 000 stroke survivors in Canada. Each year, an estimated 45 000 Canadians experience a stroke. Two-thirds of strokes hit people over age 65, and the risk of stroke doubles every decade after age 60. Medical authorities state that 30 to 35 percent of stroke survivors require continuing care when they return home.

Because Canada's population is aging, more strokes will occur. Since my father and grandfather died of stroke, I can personally attest to the value of public- and private-sector programs available to help deal with rehabilitation and care. These days, the Internet conveniently brings stroke information to you, whether it relates to information on prevention, or resources on continuing care.

The Canadian Heart and Stroke Foundation's Web site (**www.hsf. ca**) has referrals to local health-care and information providers. Health-care providers include hospitals and rehabilitation, physiotherapy, and speech therapy clinics. But if it's just preventative treatment or related information you want, the U.S. National Institute of Neurological Disease (**www.ninds.nih.gov/hlthinhp. htm**) is a resource that is comprehensive in content. It reveals new developments in treatments, provides guides, tips, and preventative measures, and offers advice related to recovery. Its links, for the most part, are credible.

Parkinson's Disease

Parkinson's Web (**pdweb.mgh.harvard.edu**) is a Web site with information such as primers on the disease and ways to spot it. Treatments are presented and online support groups are revealed. Because it's a government-sponsored site, its credibility is better than comparable sites.

Cancer

About 60 000 Canadians die of cancer each year. For older persons, the risk factors are greater, as is the need to respond with preventative care. The American Cancer Society has a Web page (**www.cancer.org**) that is a little more comprehensive in content than its Canadian counterpart. However, for locally-oriented information such as referrals to cancer treatment providers, the Canadian Cancer Society site (**www.cancer.ca**) is invaluable. Here, you can get cancer agency locations and special event information, in addition to other resources.

Another risk area for men over fifty has to do with the prostate cancer. A comprehensive resource and directory can be accessed at Prostate.com (**www.mediconsult.com/frames/prostate**). Here, you can also access online medical articles or join discussion and support groups that deal with this issue.

Practices and Professions

Another way of looking at a health-care issue is to view it from a professional perspective. This research approach will provide you with a "big picture" perspective—information about a condition, locations of practitioners, and the mandate(s) of related associations or professional colleges. The following Internet resources provide such a perspective.

Medical

If you wish to access general medical information, one site that can help is Family Internet (**www.familyinternet.com/mhc**). The links at this home page are categorized by subject: symptoms, nutrition, injury, and more. This site is ideal for obtaining timely answers to some of the more common medical questions posed by those over fifty. With over 750 000 internal pages (1 gigabyte of information), and the ability to pose an online (e-mail) health-related question to a physician, this site is likely to provide you with the information you're looking for.

Another information-oriented site is HealthFinder (**www. healthfinder.gov**). It has a storehouse of online medical publications, referrals to online support groups, and many links to other general health-related Internet resources.

Should you require information that's a bit more specific to people who are "fifty-plus", try Ask The Doctor (**www.health-net. com/seniors.htm**). In addition to actually being able to ask health-related questions online (e-mail), you can peruse previous FAQs, execute keyword searches, and scan the site's many subject listings (such as seniors' changing medical needs). If you do ask a question, replies are generally received within a few days; and your name is kept confidential.

Dental

Dental care is critical for everyone; but for those over fifty, even more so. This is the age when gum disease and other periodontal problems tend to set in. What are some of these dental complications? How are they treated? You can click into the Ask Dr. Tooth site at DentistInfo (**www.dentistinfo.com**) to find answers. Here, you can learn about the do's and don'ts of tooth and gum care by simply firing off an e-mail to an "online dentist." Or, simply browse their dental information resources.

A distinctly Canadian resource is The Tooth Fairy (**www. tootfairy.org**) where you can get information on dental and oral hygiene issues. There is a good collection of FAQs and strong links to related resources—both dental-care-oriented sites and professional (for example, dental hygienist) sites.

If you need even more dental information, try The Dental Zone (**www.dentistzone.com/dds/dds_ask.htm**). Although U.S.-based, this site is strong on generic dental information links and even maintains an online directory of U.S. and Canadian dentists. If you're a snowbird, you can get information about U.S. dental practice locations in advance of your trip south. It's one less thing to do when you arrive at your destination!

Vision

The aging process often takes a natural toll on people's eyesight. If this happens to you and you're looking for general information, FAQs, and guidelines about vision-related matters, then Internet Vision Care will probably have what you need. This resource, at **www.visioncare.com/ask.htm**, is solid in terms of being able to access additional information such as articles and other online vision-care publications. Its links are comprehensive and apply to both U.S. and Canadian audiences. A professional optometrist (in the U.S.) can even answer your specific vision-related questions via e-mail.

Psychology

If you have a psychology-related question, you can browse through Mental Health Interactive's (MHI) "Ask The Expert" pages (**www.mhsource.com/interactive**). Or, before you ask your own question, you can scan their archives for FAQs that are already posted. In addition to the site's interactivity, you can access information and educational resources on psychological disorders. This information is well-organized and well-represented at MHI. Mailing lists can also be accessed through this resource.

Alternatively, you can scan newsgroups (alt.*condition name*) to see what information other individuals have to offer, say, on the topic of grief or depression—common amongst mature persons as their friends and loved ones begin to pass away. But you may ask yourself what an isolated medium like the Internet could possibly offer someone suffering from conditions as isolating as grief and depression.

It so happens that many find the Internet to be pressure-free and without barriers when expressing true feelings. The result? Better coping. And while there will always be those on the Net writing harmful and malicious messages, many more participants will treat you with empathy and hold your hand along the way. (Perhaps a way to avoid online "predators" is to minimize one-to-one personal replies to your postings; or to share such replies with others in the newsgroup. This way, someone else watches over you.)

One last word here. Be very cautious about the quality of information on the Net, especially with newsgroups. On the one hand, the Net can be superb. The most recent advances are usually first published somewhere on the Internet. On the other hand, you'll likely run into quacks who like to play doctor in newsgroups. These are frightening people that can do you and others immense harm. Never take any such advice, especially recommendations dealing with anti-depressants or any other medication for that matter. Leave prescription recommendations to your health practitioner.

Nutrition and Diet

A proper diet is important for all age groups. But as someone over fifty, a good dietary regimen should be a critical concern to you. Older individuals sometimes skip meals altogether or mistakenly believe that they "don't need to eat as much." Notwithstanding quantity, these persons sometimes miss out on quality. The "Canada's Food Guide" is a good source of basic dietary information and is available through Health and Welfare Canada's Web site (**www.hwc.ca/datahpsb/seniors/seniors/english/ health.htm**). (More discussion of government health resources can be found at the end of this chapter.)

Yahoo (**www.yahoo.com/Health/Nutrition**) is even more comprehensive. You can click on the "Indices" link to get access to specialized directories. In addition, you can access many other sites dealing with nutrition from this Web page.

Finally, if you can't find anything in the above-noted resources, try Nutrition Centre's directory (**www-sci.lib.uci.edu/HSG/ Nutrition.html**). Here, you can access many online and offline resources. There's a useful "Consumer Information" link, hotlinks to a wealth of diet-related sites, online nutrition journals, and accessible databases of information. You can also access this directory from the above Yahoo site.

Chiropractic

Many people over fifty suffer from some back complications, or at least know someone of the same age group that does. This is natural as the spinal structure of older persons is taxed by age, posture, and just plain use! Whether or not you have back concerns, proper preventative or remedial back care information is valuable.

Because one in ten Canadians, many of these being older persons, will pay a visit to a chiropractor each year, it's always a good idea to prepare for an actual visit.

The Canadian Chiropractic Association's Chiropractic in Canada site (**www.inforamp.net/~ccachiro**) is a good site for obtaining background information or for dispelling misinformation about this growing profession. It's also ideal for browsing FAQs and for getting tips on posture and preventative back care.

The Chiropractic Page (**www.mbnet.mb.ca/~jwiens/chiro3.html**), while similar to the one above, is a little more on the technical side (geared to professionals) but may nonetheless prove useful to you, the layperson. It has links to organizations, a directory of professionals, and a list of chiropractic research materials.

Online Professional Advice

It can never be stressed enough that personal contact is irreplaceable when it comes to health-care. Even if you are not mobile, there's almost always a volunteer service near you that can get you to a health-care practitioner. However, if you seek supplementary health-care advice, you can get it through the Net.

Medical Advice from Doctors

If you have a specific medical question and want that question to be addressed by a practising physician, you can go to Drug InfoNet at **www.druginfonet.com/askmd.htm**. This health and drug information-related site allows you to make specific requests for medical advice. A certified doctor who is independent of any drug companies will answer you. Your identity remains anonymous and replies usually take about one week. You can browse through their extensive collection of medical information or you can link to other medical Web sites. FAQs in categories such as Alzheimer's and arthritis are also available at Drug InfoNet.

Because a physical assessment cannot be done through the Internet, don't interpret any online opinion obtained as being a diagnosis. Instead, treat it for what it really is—preliminary advice or a second opinion. Always remember that your likelihood of getting an inaccurate "online" opinion exceeds the likelihood of getting an inaccurate initial (physical examination) medical opinion. So opt for the physical examination whenever you can!

Psychological Advice from Psychologists

Dealing with one's psychological issues on the Internet warrants careful consideration and healthy scepticism. For every great resource on the Internet, there may be another that is a sham. In terms of the discussion that follows, I'll leave it up to you to exercise sound judgement. If you decide to use the following "advice" services, then, as a minimum, ask for a referral prior to actually using them. If neither e-mail address nor telephone number is listed on the Web site you're browsing, simply avoid these services altogether! Counselling is supposed to be a two-way exchange of information—not one way.

Professional psychologists have expanded the marketing of their practices by advertising on the Web. One professional psychologist (Dr. Leonard Holmes), at **www.psychology.com**, identifies up front the types of issues that he deals with. The list of issues is fairly comprehensive, and therapy can include individuals or groups.

Helpnet (**www.ottawa.net/~helpnet**) utilizes psychologists (all PhD's) who work as a panel and charge a fee on a per-query basis. Replies, usually received by "patients" within three days, are returned by e-mail.

There are other psychologists who ply their trade on the Net. Still more choose to simply publish information on it. A handful of dedicated volunteers have put together specialized directories to help you along on both counts. Among these directories are The

Grohol Mental Health Page (**www.coil.com/~grohol**) and Psyche Web (**www.gasou.edu/psychweb/psychweb.html#psydept**). While both are somewhat technical in terms of content, they nonetheless provide comprehensive links to various other psychology-related sites. These sites provide online articles, journals, or other sources of help.

In some ways, the electronic buffer between patient and doctor may make for a more "open" therapy. For others, lack of personal contact is anathema. As a minimum, the Net has once again allowed for one more health-care option—one that may be just what someone out there is looking for!

Online Support and Self-Counselling Resources

An online support group represents a gathering of people on the Internet that tries to deal head-on with a certain emotional, physical, or psychological problem. This problem is usually something that was experienced at one time or another by all group members. In the tradition of typical "real-life" support groups, these online groups tend to meet regularly and are a source of advice that is softer (less prescriptive) than that provided by various health-care professionals. The key advantage of support groups resides, of course, in their interactivity. Such groups also tend to be more approachable and accessible than health-care professionals, who often don't have the time to get too deeply into your concerns.

Self-help online resources, which are repositories of "apply-it-yourself" information and advice, serve to complement support groups by providing one-way information from them to you. It's one more way to help you solve a problem.

Self-counselling resources, and especially online support groups, draw on many Internet resources—the Web, bulletin boards, chat forums, newsgroups, and mailing lists. Some are free; others are fee-based.

Mental Health Net (**www.cmhc.com/selfhelp.htm**) has several internal index categories at its home page. These indices exist mainly to help you access online support and self-counsel resources. The "Self-Help Sourcebook Online" is one such index. By clicking it, you'll find referrals to many self-counsel materials that deal with emotional, physical, or psychological problems. Another Mental Health Net index is called "Psychology Self-Help." Click it and you'll find that it's very comprehensive and can help you learn more about various psychological issues, all the while providing possible solutions to cope with them. This index has over 2 000 references to many resources—so it's verifiable.

We will now look at some specific examples of the types of Internet resources you can expect to find in the area of online support.

Web-Based Support

If you ever read an Ann Landers column, liked its format, but felt that even if you wrote to the columnist you would never get a reply, a type of service is popping up on the Internet that may have what you're looking for. And it's accessible too. Under this service, the listener to your problem is someone who gives you individual attention and who is supposed to possess some type of academic credentials. Go Ask Alice (**www.columbia. edu/cu/healthwise/alice.html**) is one such service. This question-driven site (allowing you to pose questions) is a step beyond "read-only" resources such as self-help Web sites. Its online, interactive format is conducive to the fact that many specific emotional issues cannot be dealt with alone. By allowing you to ask questions, "Alice" provides very tailored responses.

The Web also supports group therapy, where you share your

problems with several other persons who in turn share their concerns with you (and others in the group). All of this is done anonymously, affording you a certain level of protection against intentional harm. You can use your search tools to find a support group by using combination keywords such as "group therapy" and "bereavement." Other keywords include "advice columns" and "online advice."

To ensure that the advice given under either approach (advice columns or group therapies) is bona fide, you should always seek references and obtain credentials from the provider of the service. If the provider denies such requests, my suggestion is to stay away from the service.

There are also specialized online support resources. Widow Net (**www.fortnet.org/WidowNet**) is one such resource. It provides information and self-help for widows and widowers to help them deal with grief, bereavement, and recovery. More resources such as these are referred to in chapter 9.

Internet Chat-Based Support

Chat groups are a little more tricky to participate in. It's PC-to-PC communication at scheduled times. You're attempting to simultaneously read what others are typing and you're replying at almost the same time. A description of IRC was provided in chapter 3, but a visit to **www.yahoo.com/Computers_and_Internet/ Internet/Chatting/IRC** can provide you with a more detailed primer.

Mailing List and Newsgroup Support

If you seek a mailing list or newsgroup (discussion group) on a "fifty-plus" support area of concern to you, the Liszt Directory of Mailing Lists and Newsgroups (**www.liszt.com**) may come in

handy. There, you'll find many pointers to health-related resources.

Drugs and First Aid—Online References

Drugs

For those over fifty, the need to take drugs may be greater than for
younger Canadians. This fact stems from the aging process and
the medical profession's prescriptive response to it. But why not
find out more about your new prescription? How does the drug
you need to take work? What exactly are the side-effects of this
drug? Answers to questions such as these can be found quickly and
easily on the Net.

One of the definitive drug-related resources is RxList—The
Internet Drug Index at **www.rxlist.com**. In it, you will find a
storehouse of information on over 4 300 prescription drugs in
the U.S. and Canadian markets. You can search the database by
brand or generic name. You can also find out what a drug's side-
effects are, what they are prescribed for, how they interact with
other drugs, and how they work. The site even contains some
drug use statistics and related trivia.

The more interactive "Ask the Pharmacist" site (**www.wilmington.
net/dees**) may also be of help. Here, you can fill out a personal
background questionnaire, pose your own personal question, and
have an e-mailed response sent back to you within days. You can
also access a good FAQ list and a growing database of medica-
tion-related information.

Remember that you should never use the Web or other Internet resource as the primary source of information about prescription
drugs. Always consult with your doctor and pharmacist about

drugs and their proper use as only they have a grip on your personal medical history. Use the Net for supplementary information only. But a key benefit of the Net remains: if a new side-effect is revealed—such discoveries occur rather frequently—about a drug you're using now, you'll likely hear about it on the Net first!

First Aid

First Aid Online (**www.prairienet.org/~cicely/firstaid**) is a repository of first aid information on topics such as breathing, shock, fainting, sprains, and bruising. It's a mostly text-based site but contains some good tips. The MedAccess site, discussed earlier, (**www.medaccess.com/first_aid/fa_toc.htm**), also has first aid resources that you can browse.

Alternative Health Care

Alternative medicine is a burgeoning industry that has found a welcoming home on the Internet. It's slowly gaining acceptance, even in the medical community. Many users of alternative medical practice are educated and affluent, contrary to the "Hollywood" portrayal of them as being "different." Both the Web and newsgroups accommodate alternative medicine information.

The Web

Yahoo seems to have its "foot" in everyone's door, and alternative medicine is no exception (**www.yahoo.com/Health/ Alternative_Medicine**).

The Alternative Medicine homepage (**www.pitt.edu/~cbw/altm. html**) is a good jump site to newsgroups, mailing lists, and related databases. It has a search tool of its own and provides links to other related Web sites as well. Shae's Alternative Medicine Pages (**users.vnet.net/shae/altheal/altheal.html**) is similar and has a fair amount of information on herbs and foods that are supposed to heal.

Andrew Weil, author of several books on alternative medicine, has set up the immensely popular Ask Dr. Weil Web site at **www.drweil.com**. It has an archive of past columns, a database of alternative medicine information, and recipes for healthy and healing eating.

Newsgroups

Newsgroup resources can be found at **misc.health.alternative** and **alt.folklore.herbs**. Searching through the **misc.health**, **alt.health**, and **alt.support** newsgroups should also yield an abundant listing of alternative health-care sub-groups.

Government Health Programs and Services

Online Information Resources

Health and Welfare Canada (HWC), Division of Ageing and Seniors (**www.hwc.ca/datahpsb/seniors/seniors/english/health.htm**) maintains a solid online collection of seniors' information on its site. HWC's general resources (**www.hwc.ca/ links/english.html**) deal with "fifty-plus" issues, health programs, healthy living, medication, alcohol, and so on. Key issues of interest to mature Canadians can almost always be found within HWC's Web pages.

In addition, you can browse the Canadian Institute for Health Information site (**www.cihi.ca**) for interesting statistics and a database of health information. This site can also be accessed from HWC.

The U.S. Administration on Ageing (**www.aoa.dhhs.gov**) has a directory of resources for older persons. It also has generic information useful for Canadians.

Using the Net for information about government health programs and services, and for accessing relevant topical discussion is cheaper and faster than the way you used to get this information before. For example, how many times have you tried to get specific program information only to be referred to someone else, or forced to weave through a maze of voice message systems?

Accessing Health Care in Canada

Although health-care is funded nationally as a universal program, it is delivered at the provincial level. Therefore, you need to know about the types of government services that are available locally. In many cases, older Canadians believe that their provincial health card and the location of their doctor and nearest hospital is all they need to concern themselves with. They simply rely on their physicians to tell them about everything there is to know in the space of a 20-minute checkup. After their check-up, they go home still unaware of the many provincial programs that exist to help them meet day-to-day health-care needs. What are these programs? How do you get more information about them?

By going to provincial government Web sites (they are listed near the end of chapter 4), you can readily access your provincial Health Ministry home page. From there, using a resident site map or index, you can peruse through their selection of programs. Some will be evident in meaning while others will be obscure. But to get detailed information about these programs, all you need to do is click your mouse and you're there! For example, the Ontario Ministry of Health has several programs that are geared to mature Ontarians. These include the Home Care, Meals on Wheels, Integrated Homemaker, and Assistive Devices programs.

In many cases, provincial health programs are cost-shared with other Ministries. For example, supportive seniors' housing and emergency eye or dental care is often cross-subsidized by various provincial Ministries. The point is that you may have to look at the Web sites of several "non-health" Ministries before you find what you want.

In still other cases, the province simply transfers funds to municipalities. To find out about these programs, you can access local Freenets (discussed in chapter 3). However, most provincial government health sites will link you to these through their own Web pages.

Government Web resources, especially in a quickly changing area such as health-care, are more up-to-date than their written counterparts—brochures. And there are no labyrinths of voice-mail or waiting lines with the Internet. In many cases, you can ask for applications directly through Web sites. Most provincial governments are doing their role in advertising their health-care programs on the Web. Your task is to seek out these resources and take advantage of them. They may very well improve your quality of life.

Chapter 7

House and Home

Housing in the retirement or near-retirement years is another important issue that anyone over fifty must deal with. When mature Canadians decide to move, it's often because of factors beyond their control, or considerations other than personal housing preference. For example, although over 90% of mature Canadians prefer (and choose) to stay in their own home, factors such as housing cost, proximity to family, and access to community services all play important parts in determining where to live during one's later years. In addition, positive or negative changes in personal finances, location of employment, health, and lifestyle options can easily trigger a move.

This chapter reveals and explores your housing alternatives in the retirement or near retirement years. Many options are presented— a few which you may not have even considered or known about.

The Internet and Your Home

The Internet has an important role to play in your housing decision. There are Internet resources to help you decide whether to move or to stay where you are. For example, with newsgroups, you can see what others over fifty are choosing as a housing lifestyle and why. The Net also helps you decide when and where to move. Many real estate Web sites exist that can show current or prospective homeowners what the housing and rental markets are doing—a key determinant in deciding when and where to move. Web sites also let you access demographic information about particular neighborhoods, towns, or cities.

The Net also allows you to see, on your PC monitor, what a particular house on the market looks like—across the street or around the world. Although you presently can't purchase a house directly through the Net, it will connect you with the brokers, vendors, or lessors of properties. You can also devise a search of online listings of homes for sale or units for rent. And if you wish to refinance that last little bit of mortgage you may still have left on your property, you can take advantage of the many mortgage calculators on the Web. To help you understand your overall housing options better, you can access glossaries of common real estate terms. You can educate yourself by perusing the many online primers on how to make or assess an offer.

The options and tools don't stop there. The Net allows you to look at housing decisions with a "fifty-plus" perspective. For example, the popularity of retirement homes and communities is growing every year and many of these can be located efficiently through the Net. In the past, many Canadians knew very little about government-subsidized housing programs because information was scarce. But with the Net, government-sponsored seniors' housing programs can be publicized another way, and therefore are more accessible to those who are "wired." You can also access free or low-cost information on housing adaptations, design, and other mobility-related issues.

Fifty+ and Still Mortgaged!

Many mature Canadians continue to carry mortgages. This should not come as a great surprise, since throughout their lives, many have borrowed against home equity (or slowed down their payments) in order to attain other objectives: getting their kids through school, traveling abroad, paying special medical costs, or providing seed capital for their businesses.

Refinancing Your Mortgage

The need to refinance a mortgage arises from time to time. Perhaps you now want to pay yours off quickly because of some extra cash that has come your way. Or maybe the interest rates have dropped so much that it's worthwhile to bail out of your existing mortgage in favour of a re-negotiated one. The Internet has resources to help you better understand your mortgage options.

Banks and Other Resources

The Royal Bank's "Reducing Mortgage Costs" page (**www.royalbank.com/english/pfs/mort3.html**) provides advice on doubling-up payments and shortening pay down periods. These Royal Bank Web pages also provide advice on whether it's better to pay down your mortgage now or stay invested in the financial markets—a hot "fifty-plus" topic these days.

CIBC's pages at **www.cibc.com**, in addition to providing you with similar mortgage-related options, has advice on what to look for in a house and other technical matters. You can even apply to refinance your mortgage online.

Remember to comparison shop at the other banks, trust, and insurance companies (some URLs were provided in chapter 4). But if you prefer a one-stop Web list of competitor interest rates, look no further than Cannex's site (**www.cannex.com**), where you will find a list of comparative rates offered at various Canadian financial institutions.

As someone over fifty, there may be a rare case when it actually makes sense for you to take on a mortgage. This may be the case when you can no longer afford "high" rent and wish to buy a smaller home (by way of preference) where your monthly payments (including mortgage and taxes) will actually be less than your rent. If you encounter this or a similar situation, visit the mortgage calculator page (click "Tools") at the Bank of Montreal (**www.bmo.com**). You can type in the amount of financing needed at a given rate and amortization period (try different combinations) and a monthly payment estimate is generated. Again, I don't recommend that anyone over fifty without other significant assets take on additional debt. It's simply too risky to do so, what with government entitlement cutbacks and the uncertain and costly medical needs that you may encounter later on.

Reverse Mortgages

Reverse mortgages are intended to help you stay at home. They do this by translating the value or equity in your home into cash. You retain ownership and residency. The cash can be received in a lump sum, an annuity, or a hybrid of the two. The amount of debt and interest that you owe increases as time passes and you will eventually have to settle this obligation—when you dispose of the home or at another time. What you do with your cash in the meantime is entirely up to you.

For more detailed "nuts and bolts" information, you can click and search through TD's site (**www.tdbank.ca**), where TD's partnership with CHIP (Canada Home Income Plan Corporation) is discussed.

It is extremely important that you discuss the technicalities of reverse mortgages with a qualified, independent financial advisor. This is a complex area with lots of variables and is certainly not suitable for everyone. Make sure that you fully understand the pros and cons—and there are always both—of your reverse mortgage options before choosing that course of action.

To Move or Not to Move—That Is the Question

Earlier, I noted a fact that really came as no surprise—older Canadians prefer to stay in their own homes. This is despite statistics that show that Canadians move more often than most people in the world. Nevertheless, controllable and uncontrollable factors often come into play. These include the ongoing cost of keeping your home, access to family, and changes in finances, employment, or health. Any one of these factors can precipitate a move.

A useful and relevant resource that can help you assess the available "fifty-plus" housing options is Eldercare Web (**www.elderweb.com**). From their index, click on "Living Arrangements" to access information on seniors' communities, home care, and long-term care facilities. There is ample discussion on the pros and cons of moving from where you now live. You can also go to their many useful links to access even more housing-related information.

A similar visit should be paid to The Guide to Retirement Living Online (**www.retirement-living.com**), where you can access information about staying at home, moving out into retirement villas or assisted/independent living providers, and even home health care. Although the site is geared to those thinking more about retirement community options (discussed later in this chapter), this Web site considers many of the key factors involved in a "fifty-plus" move.

The Senior Resource: Housing Choices site at **www.seniorresource.com/house.htm** is a "must visit" to help you deal with complex housing issues at the retirement or near-retirement stage. Good discussion and links form the foundation of this growing site.

There's also the more generic International Real Estate Directory (IRED) (**www.ired.com**). Here, you can access housing tips and online magazine articles related to seniors' housing choices and options, home adaptations, and more.

Finally, there's nothing like seeing what your peers are doing or thinking! Check out the **soc., alt.,** or **misc.** newsgroups containing extensions such as "housing," "retirement," "housing.retirement," or "retirement.communities."

Staying in Your Current Home

"Staying at home," for the purposes of the discussion that follows, can mean several things. It can involve staying in the house you are in now, remaining in the home you currently share with family or friends, or staying in your existing condominium or rented apartment. Really, it means being independent. When you "stay at home," you don't need institutional or organized assistance—although you may from time to time require "home care" visits.

A 1990 American Association of Retired Persons (AARP) study revealed that a majority of the people surveyed (86%) "wanted to stay in their present home and never move." CARP has observed similar trends in Canada where keeping one's "roots" has also been the preferred option for mature Canadians.

There are some definite advantages to staying where you are, not the least of which includes residing near the amenities and familiar surroundings of your current neighborhood. Proximity to your family and friends and the memories that your home provides you with also weigh heavily in the decision to stay at home.

Nevertheless, you have to assess the necessity of remaining in your existing home with a clear head—without excessive sentimentality. You need to address several important issues. To help you along, some of the things you need to consider are listed in the table on page 171.

Stay or Move Out? A Checklist

The current cost of keeping house and expected changes to your
cash flow

Your anticipated health and lifestyle needs several years down
the road

Your age and health

Access to family members and proximity to friends

What you think your neighborhood will look like in the future

Whether your current house is too large or too isolated

Whether you will be able to handle home maintenance

Whether the local climate is excessively cold or humid

The likelihood of a change in your property's value

Your mortgage status and property tax burden

The availability of entertainment, religious facilities, shopping, or
work

Your ability to be involved in community groups

It's also important that you are aware of your public- and private-
sector "stay at home" options. For example, many government
programs are available to help staying at home become a retirement reality for you. Public and community health programs such
as home support services, home care, assistive and adaptive devices, and hybrid services all make it easier for you to stay independent. How to access these special seniors' health programs was
discussed in chapter 6. In addition, good "Internet-assisted" management of personal finances (chapters 4 and 5) will make staying where you are a more viable option—after all, housing is, and
always will be, one of your biggest costs. You need to stay ahead of
these costs!

Finally, always peruse the resources on your local Freenet. Why?

Housing issues and options are almost always provided there; and not just the public-sector ones. It's one of the very subjects that make Freenets "tick!"

The verdict? My advice is that if you're content at home, are able to afford it, and expect to be comfortable living there in the future, making no move may be the best move of all.

Adapting Your Home for Retirement

If you decide to retire at home, and if mobility and safety are becoming more and more of a concern to you, you need to consider a few simple ways to make it—to borrow a computer term—"user-friendly."

The Canada Mortgage and Housing Corporation (CMCH) (**www.cmhc-schl.gc.ca**) has many outstanding housing publications. To access some of these information products, e-mail them requesting a free copy of their "publications catalogue." Some publications are free and others are priced to recover the cost of production only. Many are devoted to seniors' housing issues such as home adaptations, "garden suites" (additional living quarters on residential property), and related topics. Browse their "Publications" Web pages for an overview of these publications. We will revisit this site again later because their programs don't stop here!

In my first book, the *Ontario Retirement Handbook* (ECW), I provided an extensive list of home adaptive aids. A visit to a home health-care retailer will also give you a good idea as to what is available to make your home more livable and you more mobile. Even if you do move, say to a smaller home or apartment, you'll want to familiarize yourself with these products. They'll certainly improve your quality of life and personal safety. Did you know that more than 24 000 North Americans are killed each year because of home accidents; and more than 3 million become seriously hurt or disabled? These are frightening statistics that serve as a sobering reminder that home safety is a big issue for any mature Canadian.

Many older homeowners, and almost all who are over sixty-five, are on fixed incomes. However, the need to maintain a home does not disappear and the associated costs can quickly get out of control. What are you to do? You can access the Net to obtain many online tips and advice on renovating, decorating, and landscaping your home at low cost. Newsgroups are always a good resource for this type of information. When it comes to housing issues, **alt.home** can be a great place to access useful home maintenance tips. Often, the advice found there comes from seasoned tradespersons who publish novel solutions to complex home-related issues. As for the Web, you can get advice from *Hometime's* Dean Johnson at **www.hometime.com**. Text summaries of past PBS *Hometime* broadcasts can be accessed there.

Moving to a New Home

If you're planning or are compelled to move elsewhere rather than staying at your current home in your retirement or near retirement years, you should begin planning ahead. Poorly planned moves usually lead to rushed decision-making and costly mistakes. You need time to assess the alternatives available to you and to make well-reasoned, educated decisions. These are discussed next.

There are many considerations in deciding where to move to from your current home. The key moving concerns at this point involve deciding on the right time to move, the ideal location of your residence, and type of home to acquire.

The Right Time to Move

If there's one place where the Internet can really translate into dollar savings, it's the ability to make a good home sale/purchase decision based on facts and statistics accessed from the Internet. In the pre-Net days, you just never really knew if you had all the facts. When is the best time to move? Where are the hot spots? What is the housing or rental market at? To get answers, you were at the mercy of a real estate agent whose natural incentive was often the "quick sale." But this situation is different—it's a good chunk of your life savings at stake!

If you want to know if you're going to be moving during a buyers' or sellers' market, browse through CMHC's Market Reports site (**www.cmhc-schl.gc.ca/Centres/MAC/Regions**). From there, also click on "CHIC" to access fee-based material if you're really serious about demographics. With this factual, timely, and objective information in hand, you can time your move in a way that optimizes your selling price and/or moving costs.

Another repository of housing market information is the Canadian Real Estate Association (CREA) (**realtors.mls.ca/crea**). In addition to market data, it has housing tips and related news.

Finding the Right Location

Wherever you want to go, be it across the street or around the world, the Net can help you get there. But if you're considering far away places, the Net can save you hundreds of travel and research dollars.

If moving out of North America is an option for you, check out FractalNet (**www.fractals.com/outsideus.html**) to access various international listings and links. The RealtyGuide (**www.xmission.com/~realtor1**) also has a series of links to global housing-related Web resources. You can search by specific countries and regions at both of these sites. They also provide informative links, some of which let you know about a city or region's demographics, economy, and topography.

If you're thinking of a move out of Canada and down to the States, the U.S. Gazetteer (**www.census.gov/cgi-bin/gazetteer**) may be a logical starting point. You can query this resource to retrieve regional maps and demographic information for you. When you're moving far away, this sort of preliminary information is even more important than home-specific information. And if any good city in the U.S. will do, you can also check out Money Magazine's Best Places site (**pathfinder.com/@@kHUevAYANJY4@Kus/money/best-cities-96/seaindex.htm**). Here, you can rate up to 300 places on the basis of nine criteria. Finally, at Realtor.com (**www.realtor.com**) you can access over 500 000 U.S. property listings.

For Canadian snowbirds who love Florida—and there are many—you may want to peruse the South Florida Home Spot (**www.homespot.com**). If you're thinking of a more permanent move, this site will link you to other area real estate offices. Jumping from link to link, you may find yourself in any number of "Sunbelt" states of interest!

If you're flexible enough to move anywhere in Canada, the best search approach is to start with a national online housing resource—the well-known Multiple Listing Service (MLS) at **www.mls.ca/**. On any given week, there are between 110 000 and 150 000 properties listed there. This site has a very flexible search tool that allows you to select a province, city, or borough. You can also select your ideal home's features and price range. Best of all, you usually get to see a picture of the property. This site is growing fast as more and more regional real estate boards join this site. By browsing the price listings for given areas and for given types of property, you'll obtain a reasonable impression as to whether an area is good, bad, or just plain average.

Another place to go to find regional Canadian listings is the Internet Yellow Web Pages: Real Estate (Canada) at **sword.lightspeed.bc. ca/warlight/r-estate.html**. This site specializes in the Canadian West Coast. Another regional resource is the Toronto Real Estate Board's site (**www.realestate.ca**). This site attracts almost two million visits a week. Both sites provide community profiles.

As for moving to specific new cities, some of the travel-related resources (discussed in chapter 8) may actually be of help. Use these resources in tandem with those presented here to get a better "feel" for an area. Before the Net, this was difficult to do. City.net, for example, (**www.city.net**) has a "top cities" feature as well as a comprehensive listing of international (including Canadian) cities. This is a link-oriented site, so it's a general resource only. But some of these links may take you to handy local indices that include real estate agencies.

Also, check out the Seniors-Site (**seniors-site.com**). Among other topics, this evolving site will provide you with information such as "the best places to retire."

Finding the Right Home

There are many different types of homes for you to move into. And the issue of ownership has to be considered too. At this stage in life, cost, space required, and personal lifestyle preferences form your key considerations. Let's review the pros and cons of some of your options.

Buying versus Renting

Buying helps you build up equity, allows you to decorate more freely, and provides you with a principle residence tax break if you decide to sell again down the road. (The tax break is a tax exemption on capital gains made from selling your primary residence.) On the other hand, initial out-of-pocket expenses are higher when buying than when renting, maintenance is your responsibility, and you are exposed to the price and volume movements of the real estate market.

Renting keeps you mobile and there's little maintenance on your part. Monthly expenses such as water or heat are usually included in your rent, so you don't have to worry as much about usage. However, renting provides fewer tax breaks and you can't build up equity. You lack the independence of a homeowner and must generally subscribe to the landlord's rules and regulations. In many cases, you don't have gardening or pet privileges. And in some provinces, there may be few, if any, effective controls on how much rents can rise.

Buying a House versus a Condo

Houses offer you independence and all the financial benefits associated with home ownership. It's common to see older Canadians settling into smaller, less expensive homes. These individuals can enjoy more space than is found in most apartments and can delight in gardening or relaxing out on the deck. This option is ideal for active retirees who prefer maximum independence and privacy.

Buying a condominium, on the other hand, combines the benefits of owning a house with those of renting an apartment. As you probably already know, you pay a purchase price for the condominium unit itself and a monthly maintenance fee to cover common costs. But you may not have known that prices and maintenance fees vary widely amongst condominiums depending on location, size of the unit, special features, and so on. With condominiums, like houses, you are entitled to principle residence tax breaks. But with condos, you get a certain measure of flexibility (for example you can travel without leaving an obviously empty home behind) not found in houses. Condominiums, like retirement homes and communities, are conducive to socializing. Finally, a condominium is usually smaller than a house—an advantage to some!

Rental Options: Apartments versus Houses

Apartment rentals may be a good alternative for persons who want few aggravations and maximum flexibility. Local apartments are also suitable for mature Canadians who contemplate an upcoming move elsewhere and seek short-term, interim housing; or for those who are waiting for entrance into a retirement community. Also, single retirees such as widow(er)s may find that apartments offer just the right size, cost, and level of social interaction. With apartments, however, you give up flexibility.

Renting a house gives you more space, but also more responsibilities. You have to deal with maintenance and upkeep since most house rentals are through individual landlords. You may feel constrained—uneasy about hanging pictures, gardening, or doing anything that "changes" the house. This option is feasible for people seeking short-term housing, for those considering buying the house down the road, or for those who first want to see how they like a certain residential neighbourhood before they buy into it.

Newspapers are actually the best resources to find rentals. And if you're on the Internet, you can find a rental without leaving the front door! Online rental property listings can be found through the Canadian Daily Newspaper Association (CDNA) at **www. cna-acj.ca**. Here, you can access almost any Canadian daily, each with its own classifieds. Some newspapers even have search tools that allow you to enter preferred unit size, maximum rent payment, and location.

Retiring to Your Second Home

One advantage of retiring to your cottage, for example, is that you are already comfortable with it and you also know the area, neighbors, and the like. However, bear in mind that many vacation or resort areas aren't designed for year-round living—services are few and far between, shopping areas may be closed for part of the year, and recreation may be limited. Consider the availability of hospitals, restaurants, banks, and transit. Fewer people may be around, which can make you feel isolated—and less secure.

Moving with the Internet

If you're ready to move and know where and in what type of home to move into, you're poised for a real Internet treat—the ability to find a home online. You can do this in one of several ways. For apartments, you can access CDNA (discussed previously). For non-rental properties, you can browse the online listings to be discussed next. You can utilize online listings

- Before you find an agent,
- While working with an agent, or
- To list your house privately.

But before doing any of these things, physically prepare your house for quicker sale. Even a "Martha Stewart" home can be better presented! No way you say! Many a real estate agent will tell you that even the best-kept homes are sometimes poorly lit, stuffy, too cold, or too hot—something that doesn't come out in just a picture.

To ensure maximum listing value and appeal, clean up the inside of your house; touch up the exterior by painting and landscaping it; remove kitchen clutter; keep rooms well-lit; and hold a garage sale to get rid of old, unnecessary belongings that make a home look dated.

Online Listings

You may want to start your search before you find an agent. This allows you to get a "feel" for the market and reduces some of the pressure to buy quickly. The Multiple Listing Service (**www.mls.ca**) is best known for its published books or clippings of properties up for sale. Now, most of this same wealth of information is available online. It's a good resource to help you along with preliminary research. But addresses are kept confidential for obvious reasons. (To me, this is a disadvantage—I would prefer driving by a nearby house before viewing it inside.) However, this drawback is more than mitigated by the fact that you can tailor your online searches with your desired parameters for price, number of rooms, type of layout, and location. You can even find an agent at the MLS site. A similar resource is **www.realestate.ca,** where you can once again tailor your search by order of preference. It's a great research tool prior to actually buying a property.

There is one thing you should know about online listings, however—they sometimes take weeks to get on or offline. If time is a factor, hooking up with an agent is important.

Getting a Good Agent

A good real estate agent will keep your interests at heart—a bad one could severely impair your finances. Don't underestimate the importance of a good relationship. The key Internet advantage here is that you can "meet" an agent for the first time "at arms length." How? By initially contacting one by e-mail or phone and keeping it that way until you have made up a short list of agents you may want to meet in person. Most online listings (such as MLS) include the listing agent's (and broker's) name. Contact some of these—not too few and not too many.

When it's best for you, interview some. Don't go with an agent that's slow to respond to your query as this indicates that they are using the Web as an advertising medium rather than as a communication tool.

Royal Lepage (**www.royalLePage.com**), a private real estate company, has the strongest presence on the Internet. It's also expanding their "Future Link" Web application where you can view rooms inside a house in virtual reality (360 degrees)! From their site, just like at any other real estate company site, you can find a real estate agent. You can also access its U.S. Sunbelt vacation property listings—a popular Web spot for many Sunbirds.

Other agent and broker names can be found by perusing CREA (**www.mls.ca**).

Listing Your Home Privately

Selling your home privately is now a lot less intimidating since the Web can provide necessary information. The Online Real Estate Network (OREN) at **www.oren-realestate.com** allows sellers to avoid agent commissions. For a fee of a few hundred dollars, you get a one-year Web listing, four photos, and space to describe your house. Currently very small and focused on Ontario, this site is likely to expand nationally, especially if the number of private listings grow.

I Found It!

Once you have found a house, you may need some legal information. What's the land transfer tax? How does the inspection process work? What else do I need to know? At OREN's site, (**www.oren-realestate.com/ref.html**) you can access the advice of CFRB national commentator and real estate lawyer Alan Silverstein.

His best advice deals with how you can avoid costly real estate purchase mistakes. But remember, you still can't make an offer online. In the future, however, this may change.

Retirement Communities

In Canada and the U.S., there are essentially two different types of retirement communities:

- Standard communities that offer housing and recreation alone.
- Service-oriented retirement communities that offer varying degrees of service ranging from housekeeping to long-term medical care.

Standard Retirement Communities

The standard retirement community or adult-living community is a housing development geared solely to adults over a certain age, usually 50. This is the traditional type of retirement community—the sort of development that has sprung up in the retirement meccas of the U.S. Sunbelt states.

The specific type of housing found here varies. Different communities have one, all, or a combination of garden apartments, single-family houses, co-ops, or condos. In most cases, you buy your home under a standard real estate arrangement. Prices vary from $25 000 to over $1 million. In addition, you pay annual maintenance fees and often, recreation fees. Some communities allow you to rent your residence on either a short- or long-term basis.

Most standard retirement communities have recreation facilities (pools, golf courses, tennis courts) and coordinated activities. You're with your peers and you don't have to worry as much about crime and security. However, these communities are sometimes located at a fair distance from major cities. And there is limited exposure to anyone but other retirees.

Service-Oriented Retirement Communities

Service-oriented retirement communities, where costs also vary, are built to make mobility easier for their residents. The common types of service-oriented communities include independent living facilities, assisted-living facilities (supportive housing), and continuing care communities.

Independent living facilities are essentially hotels or condos designed specifically for retirees. They offer less by way of medical services and are geared for the more active mature Canadian. Costs can be high and in some cases you have to qualify by showing a certain net worth.

Assisted living facilities offer help in daily activities such as dressing, bathing, and eating. In most, a medical professional (such as a nurse or aide) is on call. Costs for assisted living facilities vary. This type of facility is best for retirees who require some assistance, but not the type of full-scale medical help required by, say, an Alzheimer's patient.

Continuing care facilities, as their name implies, provide a more ongoing level of personal care and attention. They are often referred to as "private nursing homes."

Selection Considerations

It is important that you visit a retirement home or community to establish an impression of what it would be like to live there.

Programs, costs, and sizes vary considerably. As a minimum, it is recommended that you:

- Tour all areas of the site
- Talk to other residents
- Sample the food
- Inspect the maintenance and upkeep of the premises
- Assess security
- Enquire about the proximity of churches, banks, and hospitals
- Enquire about rate structures

Internet Resources

To access a wealth of Canadian retirement communities, CARP's "Retirement Choices" pages are a good place to go (**www.fiftyplus. net**). Fifty-Plus.Net has links to many retirement communities and its site map is growing all the time. In addition, it points you to area real estate services and attractions.

The Ontario Residential Care Association (**www.orca-homes. com**) is a regional resource that allows you to get information about any one of its 300 member-facilities. These include retirement communities as well as long-term care facilities. Its site has tips on choosing a retirement community, referrals to member facilities, and links to many seniors' Web sites.

The Care Guide, another regional Web site (**www.thecareguide. com**) helps seniors and their families through the maze of care options. It points you to an inventory of retirement homes and long-term care facilities.

The Guide to Retirement Living Online (**www.retirement-living. com**) allows you to access information on U.S. retirement villas and assisted and independent living providers.

If you've got a little more cash, visit the Association of Retirement Resorts International (**www.retirementresorts.com**). You can access links to "The Worlds Most Beautiful Retirement Communities" from here.

Finally, the Retirement Net (**www.retirenet.com/aaa**) is a worldwide resource to locate retirement villas, resorts, RV facilities, vacation properties, and assisted living choices. This resource also has other links of interest to those over fifty.

Whether your financial state of affairs is solid or more tenuous, the Internet represents a "key" to your housing options. Around the world or across the block, the Net can help you with one of life's most important decisions. The growing popularity of retirement communities, and the growing number of them, is a response to the "greying" of Canada.

Government Retirement Housing Online

The Canada Mortgage and Housing Corporation's (CMHC) Web site is a "must visit" (**www.cmhc-schl.gc.ca**) if subsidized housing is something you're considering. There, in addition to their publications (already discussed) you will find a myriad of information on their programs and services. Their Web site is a great way of getting an overview on the types of housing for seniors and the disabled, how to take care of your home, ways to maintain independence through home adaptations, and how to cope at home with Alzheimer's. And is home renovation a minor issue? In 1994, almost $20 billion was spent on home renovations—more than was spent on new construction. That's about $1 925 annually per Canadian household!

In Canada, over 660 000 units of social housing are managed by provincial and municipal housing providers, or by local nonprofit organizations. CMHC supports these providers by cost-sharing these units on behalf of the federal government. CMHC's site will provide you with an overview of their cost-shared and even their unilateral (CMHC only) housing programs. A brief review of these programs follows.

Overview of Canadian Housing Programs

Government-assisted housing is rental housing where the rent is tied to your income. Any Canadian over fifty can qualify, but in most cases, priority is given to those over sixty and in greatest need. This usually means having a gross annual household income under the $25 000 range; but guidelines vary provincially. This is why it's important to also browse your provincial housing Ministry's Web pages for more specific information on subsidized housing. Again provincial government home pages can be found at **www.gov.** followed by **ab.ca** (Alberta), **bc.ca** (British Columbia), **mb.ca** (Manitoba), **nb.ca** (New Brunswick), **nf.ca** (Newfoundland), **ns.ca** (Nova Scotia), **on.ca** (Ontario), **pe. ca** (Prince Edward Island), **sk.ca** (Saskatchewan). For Quebec and the Northwest Territories, the respective Web addresses are **www.gouv.qc.ca** and **www.gov.nt.ca**. From there, an index will link you to their housing Web site.

Types of Subsidized Housing Providers
There are four general types of government-assisted housing in Canada. Some provinces have all four; others have fewer. Many of these housing options are "seniors only" or in buildings with tenants of various ages.

Co-operative Being a co-op resident means that you are a member of the co-op association. The members manage and operate the co-operative. Residents pay a subsidized "occupancy charge" (rent).

Municipal Non-Profit Many municipalities have established their own non-profit housing corporations. Check out your municipal Freenet or your provincial housing Ministry's web site for information about these local providers of housing.

Private Non-Profit These buildings are administered by private, non-profit organizations that are typically community-based. A certain percentage of the units are reserved for persons who pay geared-to-income rent.

Public Housing The provinces or their agencies typically run public housing. The building's units are usually all geared-to-income.

In many of the above cases, but especially with regards to the first three types of housing providers, the buildings are actually better constructed than those owned by many private-sector counterparts. This is because a majority of government-assisted housing groups built buildings that actually exceeded government building code standards.

Other Housing Programs

Other government assisted housing programs are available too, many delivered exclusively at the provincial level.

The Ontario Rent Supplement Program and B.C.'s SAFER (Shelter Aid For Elderly Renters) Program are examples of additional housing programs. Both are aimed at providing subsidies to persons who pay rent to private landlords. In fact, the SAFER program is geared exclusively to those over 60. Your province's Web home page will provide information as to the availability of such programs.

The Canadian Home Renewal Program (of CMHC) for the Disabled continues to be funded by the federal government and is available to all Canadians. Designed for disabled homeowners, this program also assists homeowners who have disabled dependents or family members living with them. It helps pay the costs of renovations that will make the home more accessible.

Supportive housing programs are available to those who are relatively independent but who need support services at hand on a 24-hour emergency basis. It is an alternative to long-term care facilities. Such programs typically differ from "home care" since the services are provided daily, as needed, to a number of people living in the same building. Support staff are usually on call at night in case of an emergency.

Chronic care programs are available in some provinces for those who have a health condition that is medically unstable and needs on-going attention and treatment from doctors, nurses and other health professionals. Care takes place in a hospital.

For supportive housing and chronic care, your housing Ministry or health Ministry home page will point you to such programs (and how to apply).

Be aware that waiting lists for all of the programs described in this section can be long. But again, if you plan ahead, you'll find yourself in a better position later.

Finally, don't forget to avail yourself of the many publications that can be obtained for free. The problem is that most people don't know what they're looking for since social housing is such a grey area. The solution? Browse the provinces' Web pages and find out more through their online and printed brochures. (You can request printed copies by e-mail.) British Columbia, for example, has a good collection of booklets including ones called "Accessible Housing", "BC Housing", "Fairness in Renting," and "Shelter Aid for Elderly Renters". Other provinces have similar resources in their "communications" or "publications" departments. Seek them online.

Long-Term Care (LTC) Facilities

LTCs combine housing and health-care, and are typically run by nonprofit organizations, municipalities, or private companies. Commonly referred to as "public nursing homes" (a rather narrow term), they provide for both long-term and short stay admissions.

In determining whether a place in one of these facilities is right for you, you should always consider the following four areas:

- Health care (such as doctor availability and costs).
- Physical facilities and food (including lighting, furnishings, maintenance, safety measures, and mobility enhancement).
- Quality of life (considerations such as atmosphere, friendliness among staff and residents, provisions for religious needs, social activities, recreational programs, and access to shopping).
- Administrative policies (such as attentiveness to your questions and willingness to share information).

Closing the Door on Your Housing Decision

As you can see, there are many viable housing solutions for the "fifty-plus" stage of life. Whether you choose to live in a million-dollar retirement villa, or seek a government subsidized seniors' residence, the "fifty-plus" housing issue is a bridge that must eventually be crossed—sometimes more than once. The Internet can help.

Decisions abound, even when you choose to stay where you are. The lesson? Plan ahead. Know all of your options. Pare down these options into a short list. Consider only those alternatives that meet your needs or preferences.

If you have limited resources, take a "big picture" retirement management approach, and recognize the interplay between housing decisions and your finances, health, and lifestyle.

Chapter 8

Leisure and Lifestyle

Leisure, at first glance, seems like a non-issue. But most persons in retirement or near-retirement don't give ample thought to how they use (or will use) their free time. In reality, your leisure or free time is affected by almost every major issue discussed in this book. Did you save enough money for your retirement or near-retirement leisure activities? Are you stuck needing to generate additional income at the very time you thought you'd be spending more free time with your spouse? Is your taste for leisure activities expensive or frugal? Is your health and mobility (or your spouse's) good enough to allow you to fully enjoy your favourite past times? And what exactly is leisure anyway? What are your free time options? How does the Internet fit in?

As you can see, the amount of time available for leisure is less than controllable. Yet, your choice of activities is enormous and can offset most of the constraints mentioned above. The Internet, in addition to being a great tool for helping you deal with retirement management issues—finances, generating more income, health, and housing—is a great way of revealing some new activities that you may be interested in. Perhaps worldwide travel is not as expensive as you thought. Maybe coin collecting isn't the only hobby that interests you. What exactly is that new book you were thinking of getting all about? What are other women thinking about that new fashion craze in Europe? Again, the Net brings this information to you—and it especially excels at doing this in the area of leisure.

This chapter will bring to the forefront some of the most common leisure activities associated with the retirement or near-retirement years. In addition to presenting many of the more typical leisure activities, this chapter will also demonstrate that the Net is a repository of information about lesser-known activities, interests, and preoccupations! It may lead you to the curious, the amusing, and the entertaining. Or, it can take you to the serious, the spiritual, and the deep. Leisure is about what you like. The Internet helps you better enjoy and plan your free time—retired or not. Enough said. Let's now explore.

Travel—Planning and Arrangement

Your kids are gone and you've got time to travel—at least somewhere. It could be as far away as Sumatra or as close as the town just north of where you live. But regardless of destination, you want to know more about the place before you get there. That's the planning part of the trip. You also want to know the most cost effective and quick way to get there. That's the arranging part.

The traditional way of planning a trip usually involved taking, (somewhat blindly) the advice of travel agents, friends, and travel shows. One problem with this planning approach is that travel agents are paid by commissions, which frequently depend on where they book you. Another problem is that friendly opinions are based on personal preferences that may differ from your own. As for travel shows, if you miss the show you miss out on the information!

However, before the Internet came along, you didn't have much by way of planning alternatives. With the Internet at your disposal, all that has changed. But how?

John Ripley (**jripley@island.net**), 54, and CARP member from Nanaimo, British Columbia, found that the Web provided him with many resources to help him in his quest for travel-related information:

> *I first began my access to the Internet in January 1996, at which time I was planning to travel to Costa Rica. I passed two to four hours a day following all the search results on that country and the subsequent links that are provided on most Web pages. I was amazed to discover lists of hotels, B&B's, descriptions of popular tours, and connections to travel companies in both North America & Costa Rica. Information on most countries was available that described the political situation, health risks, weather concerns, and many other factors any well-informed traveller should be aware of.*

Ripley has aptly described the comprehensiveness of the Net when it comes to addressing travel-related issues. And because the Internet is a multimedia tool, you can plan your trip with pictures, text, and sound-based information. As the clichè goes, "a picture is worth a thousand words." And as always with the Net, your information is current—especially important if you're travelling abroad where health and safety is a consideration.

Planning Your Trip

If there's one Web site that you should visit before planning your vacation, it's Travelocity (**www.travelocity.com**). That's because aside from its massive data base of travel information, it provides you with both trip planning information and trip arrangement capabilities. As far as planning is concerned, Travelocity allows you to access pictures of about 18 000 cities, resorts, and attractions. It's a truly comprehensive site.

Aside from graphics; simple, quality text content continues to be the main source of online travel information. The Rough Guide (**www.hotwired.com/rough**), Lonely Planet (**www.lonelyplanet. com**), and Fodor's (**www.fodors.com**) all provide good content with descriptions of popular world travel destinations. Fodor's even allows you to create your own Personal Trip Planner (guide) for accommodation, dining out, and sightseeing in your selected destination. It doesn't stop there. Fodors' site also contains travel and health advisories; and it's a great online repository of tips and general discussion on:

Disabilities and accessibility	Tour packages	Senior citizens discounts
Airline bargains	Jet lag	Flight cancellation insurance
Photography	Video cameras	Laptops
Travelling alone	Travel health insurance	Automobile rental
Discount clubs	Exchanging cash	ATMs
Telephones	Home exchanges and rentals	Traveller's cheques

You can download Fodor's advice and save it on your PC to read later.

Newsgroups are also good, especially if you seek opinions about certain destinations. Because the opinions and preferences posted are many, you'll likely come across some perspectives that are more like yours; thus helping you reach a better decision on destination (for example, convenience may be important to you but not to someone else). Many newsgroup sub-groups can be found under **rec.travel** and **alt.travel**. Appendix I also provides some examples of more specific newsgroups on the Net.

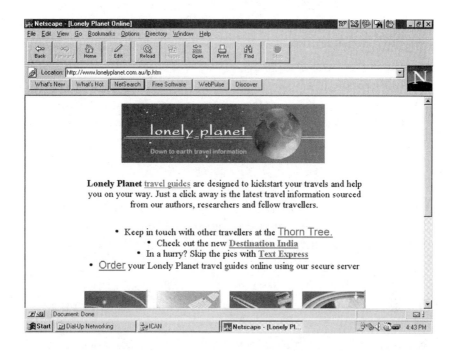

By now, you've learned that a search tool is handy, and that searching for travel destination material with one is especially handy. To this effect, try Lycos and Alta Vista—they're strongest on the local "shopping" and "dining out" side of things.

The Short List

Once you have narrowed down your search to a short list of possible travel destinations you may want to take a closer look at the specific attractions within each. There are three good approaches to help you do this.

First, use your search engine. Start by being most specific. For example, in Alta Vista (a good search engine for travel purposes) you can key in the name of your destination and add the word tourism. If nothing good comes up, enter only the destination's name.

Next, you can try going to the federal, state, or provincial government home page that relates to your destination. For example, enter "government" and the name of the destination in Alta Vista or Yahoo's search tool. Once in a government home page, look for the likeliest link to "tourism." In those pages, you may find detailed information about many cities and their attractions. (I use the word "may" because many countries have still not embraced the Internet to the extent of North America; and a hoped-for Web site may simply not exist.)

Finally, and probably your best bet, try browsing the city-oriented Web sites that are popping up all over the Web. Most have listings of restaurants, theatre, and other happenings. The Web is a perfect way to get such information because it's so current. Some of these are discussed next.

Yahoo (**www.yahoo.com**) is an important jump station to city-specific information. Their "Metros" links to cities around the world are growing by the week. City.Net (**www.city.net**) is also a comprehensive source of local city information. It has over 5 000 destinations in its database and it, too, is growing all the time. I selected Vancouver and came up with 32 relevant "brochures." The topics covered included dining, sights, sporting activities, and much more.

Infoseek (**www.infoseek.com**), another provider of city-specific resources, allows you to download street maps of a destination that interests you. In Sympatico (**www1.sympatico.ca**), click "Across Canada" in the "Around town" icon for information on Canadian happenings.

The Choice

You're almost there! You've just about decided where you want to go. But if you're thinking of travelling abroad, you still need two more important pieces of information before you actually proceed to arranging (pricing and booking) the trip. In fact, you may not have even thought about health and foreign exchange. You would typically have gotten this information from your travel agent—after the trip was booked.

Not any more. The immediacy of the Net is a perfect way to personally deal with these constantly changing issues.

At Travel Health (**travelhealth.com**) you can find useful tips on water and food screening, and disease alerts. This Web site also has generic advice on specialized topics such as travelling when you're less than perfectly mobile—a frequent "fifty-plus" consideration. The Centre for Disease Control (**www.cdc.gov/travel/travelmap.html**) has a map-driven site offering even more detailed information.

The cost of your trip depends not only on destination and preferred amenities, it also depends on exchange rates. Currency Exchange (**www.xe.net/currency**) will give you an indication of how much a currency fluctuates and will also, of course, allow you to predict how many Canadian dollars you'll need to exchange for your trip.

If you follow this approach, you are to be congratulated. When it comes to travel, there is nothing wiser than an informed consumer!

Arranging Your Trip

While you may know your destination, you still have to book transportation and accommodation. More than anything else, the cost of your trip will depend on these last two factors.

In the past, hotel prices were about the only thing you could control. But with the Internet, you can now shop for the best airfares without relying on a commission-based agent's word.

Airlines

The general consensus is that you won't save money by booking your own trip; and 85% of Internet users still arrange their actual flight bookings through a travel agent. Besides, not every airline publishes its prices on the Web. Therefore, your comparison shopping on the Net is currently limited to only a handful of useful Web sites, and so is best done by phone.

Nevertheless, sites that allow for arranging flight and other bookings (like Travelocity) do in fact save time. And as more airlines publish fare and flight information on the Web, this form of travel arrangement will likely catch on, just as ATMs (automatic tellers) did.

As for Internet resources, the Air Travellers Handbook Homepage (**www.cs.cmu.edu/afs/cs/user/mkant/Public/Travel/airfare.html**) provides a good series of links to online airline reservation systems. It also has tourism-related content and referrals to travel publications. It's packed with tips, factual information, and useful travel links.

A truly international airline travel resource can be found at **w3.itn.net/airlines**, Airlines of the Web. Here, you can obtain a list of airlines on the Web and you can also access their convenient toll-free numbers for more information

Railways

If you're thinking of touring Canada by train, or just want to puddle-hop from one city to another, VIA Resernet Interactive (**www.viarail.ca**) is the place to go. Here, you will find links to schedules, fares, tour packages, photographs, and literature. There's also a seniors' Web page link detailing the amenities and discounts offered to those over 60.

If you're transferring trains to the U.S., then Amtrak (**www. amtrak.com**) can show you their routes, schedules, and prices;

can help you make reservations; and can even give you a brief primer on the history of passenger rail travel in the U.S.

If you're railing across Europe, the European Rail System Online Travel site (**www.starnetinc.com/eurorail/railindx.htm**) has information on packages and advice on how to see Europe by rail.

Accommodation

Choosing where to stay is obviously important. You'll be spending a reasonable part of your vacation there. It should be a nice place, reasonably priced, and conveniently located.

Hotels and Travel on the Net (**www.webscope.com/travel/chains.html**) has extensive links to well-known hotel and resort chains. It's a logical starting point—but starting point to what? Once linked to a hotel or resort Web site, you'll likely be able to obtain all or a part of the following types of information:

1. Rates
2. Package deals
3. Room vacancy
4. Room type
5. Booking information

If you want more specific information, the Accommodation Search Engine (**www.netxtra.co.uk/accom**) saves you the time associated with perusing a long online list of hotels. You basically start out by clicking on a map of the world. You keep clicking until you reach a city or town. Once there, you can fill out a hotel "preference" form, where you can specify the price and amenities you're looking for.

Cruise

The Cruise Web (**www.cruiseweb.com**) gives you prices and previews of various cruise options. For example, you can choose a destination and then see which liners take you there; and for how much money. From there, you can even book the cruise and arrange it further by getting an itinerary, obtaining pricing plan information, and gathering cruise line-specific information.

Car Rental

Car rental agencies are now appearing on the Web. Alamo's Freeways site (**www.freeways.com**) has handy road travel advice and maps out for you a route within a given destination. This site is handy if you're a snowbird in the U.S.!

Bus Travel

Coach travel is still a popular way to get around, especially with relatively close or less-accessible travel destinations. Greyhound (**www.greyhound.com**) has scheduling, pricing, packaging, and booking information online. Use one of your search tools to find out if your local bus company has a Web site. Always remember—studying an online schedule of any type on your PC monitor is a lot less confusing than trying to absorb the detail by phone!

Bed and Breakfasts

Bed and Breakfasts (B&Bs) are enjoying increasing popularity with mature Canadians. One online resource is The Internet Guide to B&Bs (**www.traveldata.com/biz/inns**). It's handy if you seek information on B&B locations, services, and costs. It's U.S. in scope has several links to Web sites developed by B&Bs. Check out Yahoo for even more directories of B&Bs around the world.

Recreational Vehicle (RV)

To put it simply, RV sales are skyrocketing. In 1996, North American sales of RVs hit a record $12.4 billion. Over 450 000 new RVs were sold in that year. What is even more stunning is the fact that the used RV market is three times bigger than the new RV market! Whether it's a pop-up model or a "road yacht," this mode of travel has always been a "fifty-plus" favourite! (But let it be known—boomers are catching on fast!)

RV Link (**www.rvlink.com**) is one of the most comprehensive resources, giving you RV dealer (new and used) and RV camp site locations. Also, you can rent an RV through here. Although U.S.-based, this site is handy for any Canadian RV enthusiast.

The Elderhostel Option

Elderhostel (**www.elderhostel.org**) is an organization that helps you learn about and access reasonable accommodation at relatively low cost. It is a popular option with persons over fifty who are on fixed incomes. With Elderhostel, you can still go to far-away places, embarking on a good selection of educational and adventurous programs. Although rooms and bathrooms are typically shared, and although accommodation is often in a non-hotel environment, you can really save on travel costs.

Another "alternative" travel option is World Wide Travel Exchange (**wwte.com**), where you can link to resort villa and home exchange Web sites.

Travel Packages: An Offline Approach

We've seen how the Net can be useful in helping you to plan and arrange a trip by yourself. If you prefer, you can fall back on a more traditional information gathering approach, where packages are simply "advertised" through the Internet medium.

CARP is a conduit to member discounts on travel and insurance products and services. Clicking on Fifty-Plus.Net's "CARP Travel" icon will provide you with information on air, coach, and tour packages to many destinations. Similar member discounts can also be obtained if you require travel insurance.

And don't forget travel agencies. Many now have Web sites that can be accessed with a search tool. It's one more effective way to get travel package information.

What Are Your Peers Doing?

You may be wondering what others over fifty do vacation-wise. According to a U.S.-based study, the number of mature North American vacationers and travellers is increasing steadily, currently representing 30 percent of all travel. From 1985 to 1990, the number of vacations or trips taken by seniors jumped from 111.7 million to 152.1 million. Also, seniors account for 32 percent of all hotel room-nights.

Also according to the study, the eight most preferred types of trips (international or domestic) among the "fifty-plus" group are:

1. Waterfront sunspot
2. Travel abroad and tours
3. Cruise
4. Mountains
5. Resort
6. Theme parks
7. Fishing
8. Driving tours

Shopping on the Net

A common assumption made by many Internet users is that shopping through this medium will automatically produce large discounts for them. This is only true some of the time. And many Internet vendors have not yet come to grips with the fact that most buyers are unwilling to pay a premium for the privilege of shopping online, especially after having invested significantly in computer equipment and online hookups. Yet, some online vendors are simply too small to generate enough of their own purchasing power; so they're unable to pass on any discounts to their online customers.

You should also know that many "traditional" retailers who also advertise on the Web still cannot match the depth of product lines offered by catalogue-producing counterparts. Therefore, as a potential online consumer, you should make sure that you've considered all of your purchase options—meaning non-Web options too.

So what do you do? As a consumer, you should follow these guidelines listed in the table below before buying anything on-line:

Online Shopping Guidelines

Price the same online product with its catalogue or retail counterpart to make sure it's at least 15% to 20% cheaper. (Online ad savings ought to be passed on to you.)

Make sure that product descriptions are clear enough to allow you to make an informed decision.

If the picture of the product is poor, don't buy it.

Make sure that the site offers some assurances about quality and that brand-name items, which usually come with guarantees, are carried within the vendor's product line.

For electronic malls—sites that merge together an assortment of online retailers—scan the home page for assurances that vendors are expected to meet quality standards.

If a site is not easy to use (for example, if it requires too much pointing and clicking to find what you want), avoid the site. After all, convenience and ease of use is the reason behind shopping online in the first place!

If you have a question (perhaps about return policies and guarantees) that cannot be answered online or otherwise, you should avoid the purchase.

Consider using the online shopping alternative if your mobility is restricted.

Remember that the onus is on the online vendor to provide you with the information and prices that will attract you to their site. And if the above guidelines are not dealt with in a satisfactory manner by the vendor, then you should avoid doing business there.

The Survey Says!

The 1996 AC Nielsen/Nordicity survey of Internet users (**www.nordicity.com**) found a surprising statistic—Internet shopping (commerce) was growing at a rate faster than the Internet itself. Also, 11 percent of users have already made a purchase (seven percent in 1995) and 37 percent stated that they are likely to make a purchase at some time. Over 80 percent of those that have already made an Internet purchase stated that they would do so again. But why, despite this pent-up interest and apparently positive experience with online shopping did only one in ten persons actually buy a product or service?

Online security appears to be the key concern. People want "others" to test it out first. They want assurance that security is airtight. My advice to you? Wait a few more months. See if this new and supplemental way of shopping evolves even more as time passes. Observe if there are any "horror" stories reported in the news. If you don't hear any such stories, it's a good bet that things are working out fine after all!

The table below, an extract from the AC Neilson/Nordicity survey, provides some interesting insights into which categories of Net-based purchases online users see themselves making—purchases where it doesn't matter that "physical" browsing is substituted with "virtual" browsing. The findings below seem to exude a "fifty-plus" message: the top applications of Internet shopping tend towards leisure-oriented products and services. The lesson? Explore cautiously, but don't ignore.

Industries Where Goods and Services Are "Likely to Be Purchased" on the Internet

Industry	percent(%)
Computer hardware, software, and services	42
Travel information and publications	39*
Airline reservations	35*
Entertainment/culture	33*
Books and magazines	31*
Banking and investment at home	30*
Education	28
Toys and games	26
Professional training and seminars	24
Real estate	20

Source: AC Nielsen/Nordicity 1996 Canadian Internet Survey
Note: * denotes areas of traditional interest to retirees (e.g. leisure)

Online Malls

As always, a directory is a good first stop. The All Internet Shopping Directory (**www.webcom.com/~tbrown**) has a "best of" format. Hundreds of Web referrals are arranged by category. Both products and services are listed. Another directory is the Galaxy Mall (**www.galaxymall.com**), where categories are "exploded" into even greater detail. Additional directories include the Mall of Malls (**www.westcomm.com/westpg10.html**), Malls.com (**malls.com**), and Web Warehouse (**webwarehouse. com**). Some directories have search tools too.

The iMall (**www.imall.com**) promotes itself as being the "largest retail mall Web site," embracing over 1 000 stores. This site is a good illustration of what a typical Internet mall looks like.

Free Stuff!

Ok—so little in life is free. Usually, when someone wants to give you something, they want something in return. Sounds cynical? Take the case of free samples; the provider of these wants you to turn into a regular customer. The provider experiences short term pain for long-term gain. If you feel that such arrangements represent a fair exchange, then the Internet has plenty of "free" stuff for you. Should you run into such a site, you'll probably be asked for some information in return. If it's basic, such as your name and address—fine. Just make sure that you don't give out any sensitive personal information like religious or political affiliation, social insurance number, age, or, of course, credit card number.

The URLs listed below are intended to point you to examples of the types of free things you can get on the Net. Some sites are huge indices of free software. Others are corporate-sponsored Web sites.

Some Free Stuff on the Net

FreeWay	**www.vivanet.com/~woodj/money-mart/ freeway/freeway.html**
Jumbo Freeware	**www.jumbo.com**
Windows95.com	**www.windows95.com**
CraftNet Village	**www.craftnet.org/prime/freestf2.htm**

Hobbies and Special Interests

Mature Canadians often have more time to indulge in hobbies. And for those close to retirement, with the kids grown up, spending some decent time in a specific enjoyable activity becomes even more of a possibility.

The Internet can let you access hobby-related information as well as fellow hobbyists themselves. It introduces a whole new way of indulging in your hobby. How? People around the world participate in hobby and special interest newsgroups, mailing lists, and Web pages. These resources contain various forms of descriptive and useful information about many hobbies. Some sites are for novices, and some are specialized sites dedicated to serious hobbyists. Internet hobby and special interest resources can be comprehensive, company-sponsored endeavours; and other resources may be small, individual-developed efforts. Not all are free. Even if you are an expert in your hobby, there is likely even more relevant information that you can access. The Internet affords you the opportunity for continuous learning.

That's all you need to know from me. Only you know what you like. But to start you off, I've listed a few select Internet hobby and special-interest resources that typify the kinds of things you can expect to find online. The titles are self-evident and I didn't provide detailed descriptions of the sites. When you get there, most of them offer all the information you need to know. But these sites, while not the only "good" ones, are the better of their class. This means that they contain good interactivity, immediacy, content quality, and multimedia. And they're just a fraction of what's out there! Using search techniques you have already learned, (such as category indices, search tools, etc.), you can easily find more of what really interests you. Also remember that many hobby Web sites will contain hyper-links to related sites.

Finally, don't forget specialized directories, the links to which can be found in many hobby and special interest Web sites. Yahoo (**yahoo.com**) has over 2 250 entries under "Hobbies" (a subdirectory of "Recreation"). From Yahoo, you can access many specialized directories, too numerous to mention here.

Selected Hobby and Special Interest Resources

The Outdoors and Beyond

NASA Home Page	**www.nasa.gov**
Views of the Solar System	**bang.lanl.gov/solarsys**
The World Weather Guide	**www.world-travel-net.co.uk/ weather**
Storm Chaser Homepage	**taiga.geog.niu.edu/chaser/ chaser.html**
Master Gardener	**gopher://leviathan.tamu. edu/11s/mg**
Garden Web	**www.gardenweb.com**
Garden Net Web	**trine.com/GardenNet**
Gardening newsgroup	**rec.gardens**

Closer to Home

Collector's Coin Universe	**www.coin-universe.com/ index.html**
American Numismatic Association	**www.money.org**
Trading Cards Price Guides	**www.wwcd.com/priceg/tcpg.html**
Stamp Universe	**www.stampworld.com/index.html**
Model Railroads newsgroup	**psu.org.model-railroad**
Woodworking newsgroup	**rec.woodworking**
The Wine Page	**www.speakeasy.org/~winepage/ wine.html**
Epicurious	**www.epicurious.com**
Mimi's Cyber Kitchen	**www.smartlink.net/~hiller/food/**
Copycat Recipes	**www.copyKat**
Cooking With Caprial	**www.pacificharbor.com/pubmkt/cc**
Sally's Place	**www.bpe.com**
Recipe newsgroups	**alt.creatIve-cooking, rec.food. cooking, rec.food.recipes**
Electronic Gourmet Guide	**foodwine.com**

Harry Gilman, 54, (beckbear@istar.ca), is an Internet enthusiast and provides the following additional advice and observations.

I have become addicted—if addicted is the right word— to the fun, practicality, and convenience of the Internet. I use the Net to pursue hobbies such as writing and gardening; to plan vacations; to maintain contact with friends and relatives; and to watch the latest Mars and other pictures from NASA. I am currently doing some renovating (another hobby of mine), and want to incorporate an Art Deco theme into my house. A few minutes on the Net and I found a wealth of information about furnishings and objects for sale.
I have discovered the world of search engines and find this to be my best source for navigating the Internet. This is not just for hobbies, but for other areas as well. All I do is provide information to one of my favourite search engines (www.pacprospector.com) and let it "surf" for me to find what I want.

Gilman offers an important final reminder: never forget your search tools or directories!

Sports and Outdoor Recreation

The Internet is an outstanding resource to find more information about your favourite sport or recreational activity. Think about it. In the case of professional sports, you want scores and results— current results. The up-to-date nature of the Internet makes this possible. In the case of professional sports franchises, many teams are now broadcasting their games on the Net—in audio and video! This means that you may be able to catch an English soccer match or an NFL game in your area—through your PC. If you're in an isolated retirement community, this is a real advantage and could cost a lot less than a satellite dish.

With the Internet, you can interact with others to see how they view your favourite sport or recreational activity. You also have the opportunity to learn more and to better your skills.

Without further ado, I will list some of the more popular (well-visited) Web sites for sports and outdoor recreation information. Again, the site names are self-explanatory in terms of content. Most of them have good discussion, engaging images, audio, and a good level of immediacy and interactivity.

Selected Sports and Recreation Resources

Sports

Baseball newsgroup	rec.sport.baseball
Basketball newsgroup	rec.sport.basketball.pro
Bowling newsgroup	alt.sport.bowling
Courtside	www.tspnetwork.com/courtside/homepage.html
ESPNET SportsZone	espnet.sportszone.com
Figure Skater's Page	www.webcom.com/dnkorte/sk8_0000.html
Football newsgroup	rec.sport.football.misc
GolfWeb	www.golfweb.com
NHL Open Net	www.nhl.com
NFL Info Web	www.cs.cmu.edu/afs/cs/user/vernon/www/nfl.html
NFL.com	www.nfl.com
Official Site of Major League Baseball	www. majorleaguebaseball.com
Skating newsgroup	rec.sport.skatlng.ice.figure
Ski Areas Information Center	www.travelbase.com/skiareas
SkiCentral	skicentral.com/skireports.html
SKInet Canada	skinetcanada.ca
Snow Link	www.snowlink.com

SoccerNews Online	**www.csn.net/~eid/soccer**
Stadiums & Arenas	**www.wwcd.com/stadiums.html**
Tennis ONE	**www.tennisone.com**
Tennis Country	**www.tenniscountry.com**
TenPin World	**www.shef.ac.uk/~sutbc**
The Canadian Ski Council	**www.skicanada.org**
The Sports Network	**www.sportsnetwork.com**
Valvoline's Indy 500 Home Page	**www.valvoline.com**

Recreation

All Outdoors	**www alloutdoors.com**
Boating	**wmi.cais.com/www/boating/ index.html**
Fishing newsgroup	**rec.outdoors.fishIng**
Great Outdoor Recreation Pages	**www.gorp.com/**
Hiking And Walking Homepage	**www.teleport.com/~walking/ hiking.html**
The Backcountry Home Page	**io.datasys.swri.edu**
The Birdfeeder	**www.sover.net/~terrapin/ birdfeed.htm**

For Her Eyes Only

Women are on the Net in full force! And their use of it is growing steadily. Currently, about 43% of Net users are female. And recently, their share (as compared to males) of Internet use has been growing at a brisk pace. The "1996 Canadian Internet Survey" at **www.nordicity.com/communications/charts.htm**, includes a detailed and interesting year-to-year chart that bears these facts out. These statistics mean that any person or organization providing content of interest to women is addressing an important demographic, and this population has a specific set of needs. More importantly, it means that women themselves are recognizing the usefulness and other positive attributes of the Internet.

This section will list some of the growing number of quality Internet resources devoted almost exclusively to women's issues. That is not to imply that issues discussed previously in this book—finance and health for instance—aren't womens' issues. They are—and in a major way too! It's just that this area of the chapter will have a decidedly womens' focus.

Womens' Issues

What are womens' issues? Simply stated, they are the needs and interests of women. Needs can revolve around personal finances, career, and health-care. Interests can encompass cooking, shopping, literature, house and garden, entertainment, fashion, and other lifestyle areas—many already mentioned in this chapter. In other words, any need and interest, when viewed through a woman's perspective, is a womens' issue!

But not all womens' issues are as innocuous as those mentioned above—especially when they concern women over fifty. As Canadian women age, different types of serious concerns come to the fore. The information below outlines some of these more consequential matters. The purpose of this section is to demonstrate how online womens' resources can be applied to address or mitigate their present or potential concerns. Some of these on-line resources are discussed here. Others are found in various chapters in this book.

Issues Faced by Mature Canadian Women
Health Considerations Women in Canada live longer than their male counterparts. In fact, a recent Statistics Canada survey has revealed that this gap has widened. That's the good news if you're

a woman! But this trend obviously doesn't preclude you from having health problems of your own. Conditions such as heart attacks and osteoporosis often prove to be much more problematic for women than for men. Good health, and the maintenance of it, is a significant issue for all older women.

Need for Public Benefits More mature Canadian women than men live in poverty. Older women are almost twice as likely as older men to be living this way. Many mature women rely on government programs and cash entitlements. Many also rely on subsidized housing and basic health-care. Some lose out on benefits because they don't know about them. All seniors, and especially women, need to be informed about programs and services available to them.

Limited Employment Opportunities It's frustrating enough that women of any age group tend to run into pay inequities. But women over fifty don't even get that far—the doors are shut before they can even get into a workplace. They're all too often discriminated against by virtue of gender and especially age. Although there are strategies to overcome this (discussed in chapter 5 of this book), this is a formidable womens' issue, especially in this era of government pension cutbacks. Mature Canadian women need re-employment strategies.

Fewer Financial Planning Skills Many mature Canadian women, especially widows, lack key financial planning skills. Without these skills, they are placing their financial independence at risk. Many women over fifty need to enhance their financial planning and cash management skills.

Inadequate Housing As they age, women are more likely to live alone. But as the size and maintenance of a home becomes problematic—physically and financially—older women need to know their housing options (such as those discussed in chapter 7).

Caregiving Commitments Women over fifty provide the majority of family caregiving in Canada. They care for ageing parents, unwell husbands, or even grandchildren—at least some of the time. They need information about respite and other health-care programs.

Stressful Periods of Time Women are especially vulnerable during life changes such as divorce and widowhood. They need information about their entitlements and their rights. They need information about support groups.

Concerns over Personal Safety Fortunately in Canada, our crime rates are not as high as elsewhere. However, crime can happen anytime and anywhere. This is especially true for older women, who are the primary targets for commercial fraud and other scams. And they're more than twice as susceptible to elder abuse. Senior women need to access more advice on personal safety. (Relevant fraud and safety-related resources are discussed in chapter 9.)

How Can the Internet Help You Deal with Womens' Issues

Many of the serious issues just outlined are gender-specific but income-neutral. In other words, your level of income does not exempt you from these problems—especially those dealing with health. Equally regardless of your income status, you can access Internet resources to help you find solutions. You don't even need to buy a PC—access to the Net is free. How? Most libraries will provide you with free Internet access time. You may even be reading this book by having borrowed it from a library!

If your income is tight you can browse the Web for information about government programs, new developments in health-care, advertized jobs, housing options, caregiving tips, and personal safety.

The Lighter Side

If you're not facing any of the serious issues mentioned above, there are many other women-specific topics on the Net—topics that fortunately extend beyond information for basic survival. The discussion that follows presents Internet resources for mature Canadian women of all income groups and in many life situations.

There are lots of sites geared to women of all ages. Of these sites, most also address issues that are relevant to women over fifty. The following discussion will focus on such sites.

Sites Galore!

One distinctly Canadian womens' resource can be found at Sympatico's "Beatrice's Web Guide (BWG)—Only the Good Stuff" (**www.bguide.com**). It has strong content and a good selection of links to magazines and other womens' Web sites. BWG even supports a chat forum where "fifty-plus" women's issues can be discussed on the Net with peers.

Womens' Wire (**www.women.com/guide**) is a very popular site. Its content includes news, style, work, health, finances, and shopping. Content is truly comprehensive and the site is worth a visit. WWWomen (**wwwomen.com**) is actually a womens' Web site directory. It strikes me as being a kind of womens' "Yahoo directory." You can access resources on arts and entertainment, education, health, business, recreation, and shopping. It also provides you with online publication access.

Many women run their own small business—many "over-fifty" women. These women have acted on their need for extra income or their desire to be "busy and about." A good resource for these individuals is Engender Magazine (**www.cadvision.com/ffap/ engender**). Here, you can tap into an online forum with your peers or read interesting online articles. And the online business information content is comprehensive. It includes advice on financing, legal considerations, franchising, and starting-up a business.

The table on page 216 lists specialized Internet directories for women. It's basically all you need to access womens' Web sites and other online resources.

Womens' Internet Directories	
WWWomen	**www.wwwomen.com/**
Yahoo	**www.yahoo.com/Society_and_Culture/ Gender/Women**
	www.yahoo.com/Social_Science/ Women_s_Studies
	www.yahoo.com/Health/ Women_s_Health

Veterans' Issues

Many Canadian "senior" seniors remember World War II. Others persons over fifty remember the Korean war. Still others may have been involved in the Gulf War. Perhaps it's something best forgotten. But you should know that there are many Web resources dealing with the issues of war, the military, and veterans. Even if you were not involved in a war, you may be intrigued by it. The abundance and popularity of war documentaries on TV is testimony to that.

The definitive Canadian veterans' site is sponsored by Veterans' Affairs Canada (VAC) (**www.vac-acc.gc.ca**). Here, you can access records of fallen comrades, memorial tributes, and historical facts. You can also listen to the wartime experiences of other veterans—in RealAudio! The interactivity doesn't stop there. With their virtual reality application, you can "navigate" the Grange Tunnel at Vimy. VAC also has excellent links to related sites. Government benefit and entitlement information (such as disability, allowance, health-care, and pensions), and veteran-related information and advice can all be accessed from VAC's site and links. And links to World War I, museum, memorial, and veterans' group sites are plentiful. Of course, the location of your nearest VAC office and key contacts are available here too.

The Royal Canadian Legion (RCL) at **www.legion.ca** is another highly interactive veterans' site. From it, you can access information related to veterans' services, local legion contacts, and legal information. Its key feature, however, is that it maintains an online network of member contacts. The RCL has always represented a strong network for Canadian veterans, an its foray into a resource as interactive as the Internet comes as no surprise.

The World War II site (**192.253.114.31/D-Day**) has photographs and extensive archives of information about World War II. You can access government document extracts, speeches, and battle plans. News-reel footage of Allied and Axis forces can be viewed in the Quick Time application. The resident FTP link can also take you to map, sound, and photograph-based Internet resources.

For discussions of veterans' issues, newsgroups such as **soc.history. war.misc** represent an excellent interactive resource. Forums such as newsgroups are very conducive to the sharing of very deep, personal, and supportive messages. You may even inadvertently find a long-lost war-time acquaintance or friend through this resource.

History

The Web is rife with online historical information. And it's fortunate that the Web is so fluid because history does change after all! Historians are always coming across new revelations about things that happened in the past. These current revelations change our interpretation and understanding of past historical events.

The Internet keeps you abreast of these discoveries. With fascinating Internet facts and multimedia to further enhance your historical research, you are set to enjoy a better, more current "historical" experience. So put the history books aside, and let's visit some history-specific Internet resources!

From Past to Present

The Canadian Heritage Information Network (**www.chin.gc.ca**) provides Canadian cultural information and links to other sites, as well as historical exhibit guides. Pointers to Canadian museums are also given. If you enjoy Canadiana, this site is for you.

The History section of the Web Virtual Library (**history.cc. ukans.edu/history**) points you to well-organized online historical resources. Categories that you can search include eras, areas of the world, and other informative history topics.

The U.S. Holocaust Memorial Museum (**www.ushmm.org**) has a Web site that contains a substantial data archive and links to related sites.

U.S. Civil War Center (**www.cwc.lsu.edu/civlink.htm**) is American in content but nonetheless elicits interest from many Canadians—especially veterans. Maps, diaries, archived war information, and related links can be found at this comprehensive site. (War-related Web resources—mostly Canadian in tone—are also presented in the Veterans' Issues section of this chapter.)

Victorian Web (**www.stg.brown.edu/projects/hypertext/landow/ victorian/victov.html**) has era-related information on topics such as religion, literature, science, arts, and other issues of that time period. Speaking of Victoriana, the British Royal Web Site (**www.royal.gov.uk**) is a worthwhile visit if you're interested in the history (and current happenings) of the British monarchy. Information about the Queen, succession rights, family trees, royal finances, and related information can all be found here.

And we thought that the Royal family was running away from publicity!

The Worlds of Late Antiquity (**ccat.sas.upenn.edu/jod/wola.html**) has information on Mediterranean history that goes quite a long way back in time. Search engines and texts of ancient writings are available at this resource.

Again, if you're after any history-specific Web information (such as the history of France or the history of democracy), use search engines and directories to conduct these searches. History-related keywords may include "history" followed by the name of a country, continent, era, race, or any number of other relevant topics. Information on various historical matters can also be accessed in newsgroups. The newsgroups **soc.history** and **soc.history.moderated** may be good starting points. You can get good leads to some very specific, hard-to-find historical material here that traditional, non-Internet methods cannot accommodate. Use Liszt of Newsgroups (**www.liszt.com/news**) to help you access the wealth of history-related newsgroups.

Volunteering

Because over one third of Canadian volunteers are seniors, this is definitely a "fifty-plus" topic worth visiting. And as volunteerism in Canada continues to rise (a fortunate response to recent government program cutbacks), the role that mature Canadians have to play is even more significant. Without volunteers, many of society's needs would go unmet.

Before and after the Internet

Prior to the Internet becoming a powerful information-gathering tool, volunteering typically involved reading straightforward volunteer ads in your local paper or going to a volunteer centre. Then, you simply took what they offered you. Simple? Yes. Flexible? No!

In many cases, volunteers were matched to tasks that did not take advantage of their skill sets and experiences. This happened because, for the most part, their choice was limited to the menu of volunteering options given to them at the time. Does this process really appeal to you? After all, if you're going to donate some of your leisure time to a volunteering endeavour, don't you want to volunteer for what you really want to do and what you'd be especially good at? Absolutely!

The Internet makes it easier for you to "advertise yourself" as a volunteer. This is in contrast to the former method of simply "presenting yourself" as a volunteer. Suppose you possess skills as a word processing software trainer and educator. Why not send out quick and efficient e-mails to non-profit organizations that may need to update their staffs' PC skills but don't have the resources to train or update them? These organizations may very well take you on as a "technical" volunteer. Or, if you have business experience, why not become a volunteer consultant! It's a great way to keep busy and to stay involved in the business world. You can share your knowledge with those who need it most.

Why Volunteer?

Volunteering is a very personal decision. It is triggered by both desire and, at times, need.

Personal Satisfaction
People volunteer for many reasons. In the case of many mature Canadians, it's a constructive use of time and a great way to impart a lifetime's worth of skills, talents, and experiences to others.

Other reasons for volunteering include the opportunity to engage in more social interaction, the sense of giving back something to the community, and the chance to experience the warm feeling associated with helping others.

Upgrading Needed Skills

Volunteering is also a great way to upgrade your skills. If you've been out of work and need to supplement your income, extra skills are usually what's needed to get your foot in the "employment" door. Without these extra skills (like computer skills), you may be locked out of the job market for good. As I mentioned in chapter 5, it's tough enough getting a job as a mature Canadian with age discrimination being a problem everywhere. Don't allow this door to be shut. At least not easily! By upgrading your skills through volunteering, you have a very good chance of getting back to work.

Who Do I Turn to If I Want to Volunteer?

Traditional avenues to volunteering include visiting a volunteer centre (using your telephone directory to find them) or reading community paper ads. Another way is by contacting organizations by phone about such opportunities.

Internet-related avenues also exist and the Net happens to be extremely well-suited to providing local volunteer opportunities to people. Opportunities would most likely be presented within a municipal Web site, rather than as a site in its own right.

Advertised Opportunities

- Check your local Freenet and bulletin board. You can obtain the Freenet address and login details from your local library or city/municipal/town hall.
- Use an Internet directory (like Yahoo) or search tool (like

AltaVista). Enter keywords such as "Yourcity + volunteer," or variations thereof. Narrow it down to the local level if you can.

Self-Created Opportunities

- If the organization (commercial, public, or non-profit) you wish to volunteer with is not on the Net, use Sympatico's Canada411 link (**www.sympatico.ca**) to get a telephone number. Then, phone them up and talk to someone about your willingness to volunteer your services.
- Another alternative is to use Infospace (**www.infospace.com**) to get the e-mail address of an organization where you would like to volunteer. Send an e-mailed "request to volunteer." The message should be brief and less formal than a résumé. Don't forget to state your area of interest.

What Can You Do?

One thing to keep in mind is that even with volunteer positions, you still have to be qualified to a certain degree. It depends on the position. This is good, however, as it will ensure that volunteerism continues to be a credible option and that volunteers are afforded the respect that they deserve. The table below outlines some popular areas that many "fifty-plus" and other volunteers are leaping into these days.

Volunteering Options
Children and teens (foster grandparent)
Disabled persons (individually or through a volunteer program)
Persons recovering from drug and alcohol abuse
Educational institutions (tutors, mentoring programs)
Health-care facilities (hospitals, clinics)

Housing, poverty, and environmental advocacy groups
Political parties (canvassing, fund raising, or administration)
Professionals (medical and legal administrative assistance)
Professional experience-sharing (business start-up assistance
programs sponsored by governments)
Radio and TV stations (programming administration)
Seniors' groups (CARP, Grey Panthers, and Seniors for Seniors,
etc.)
Seniors programs (meals on wheels, wheels to meals, senior
companion, long-term care facility assistant)
Service clubs (Rotary, etc.)

Arts and Literature

You, like others, probably like to explore the finer things that life has to offer. You know what areas you like and you don't need me to describe them to you. So I'll get right down to them—to what I believe are the better Internet sites dealing with "Arts and Literature."

General Arts Resources

Index-type resources are always good starting points. Some of these are listed next.

ArtSource (**www.uky.edu/Artsource/artsourcehome.html**) is a selective, "best of" site that can link you to online art exhibits, architectural resources, image collections, museums, and more. It's a good jump station to any art form in general.

World Wide Arts Resources (**wwar.com/index.html**) is another, more specialized gateway and search tool that lets you access over 3 000 categories of art including performing arts, museums, galleries, and other art forms. Over 150 000 pages, contained within an expansive database, can be searched here.

Arts Net Homepage (**artsnet.heinz.cmu.edu**) is a useful, centralized repository of general arts-related information. It provides easy access to arts and cultural information. It's worth a stop if you're really into the arts.

Museums and Art Galleries

Almost every major museum in the world has a Web page. That's the good news. The unfortunate news today is that a majority of these only provide online brochures and basic information. Nevertheless, many still provide excellent online exhibits that you can view on your PC screen. Some of these better ones are presented next.

First Stops
Finding a museum Web site is quite easy, especially if you know its name. But even if you don't, a good place to start is Yahoo (**www.yahoo.com/Arts/Museums_and_Galleries** and **www. yahoo.com/Arts/Museums_and_Galleries/Exhibits**). Because art is such a personal affair, it does you little good if I present sites that I think would interest you. What you really need to know is how to find them. You need to be familiar with key online museum and gallery directories, such as the one above.

Canadiana

The National Gallery of Canada (**national.gallery.ca**) is a growing site that continues to expand its collection of Web photos of actual gallery displays. It also includes exhibit dates and other details of interest to potential visitors.

The Canadian Museum of Civilization and Canadian War Museum (**www.cmcc.muse.digital.ca**) and The Royal Ontario Museum (**www.rom.on.ca**) allow you to browse through their online collections. Their selection of images is good; and like the National Gallery of Canada, their sites are expanding in variety.

Famous Places and Things

The Metropolitan Museum of Art (**www.metmuseum.org**) is one of the world's largest, finest, and most famous museums. It has over 2 million artworks encompassing 5 000 years of history. This site provides you with a solid overview of their collections.

The Dead Sea Scrolls site at **sunsite.unc.edu/expo/deadsea. scrolls.exhibit/intro.html** has some one of my favourite pages to browse through. These documents have changed the course of history, so don't you think their own history is worth reading? At this site, you can get background information and you can view scroll fragments and artifacts relating to them.

The Smithsonian Institute is certainly a famous museum. Its site (**www.si.edu**) offers online tours of parts of its real-life exhibits. If you're tired of keyboarding, not to worry—this site will read to you too!

Paintings

Online Art Resources (OAR) (**www.msstate.edu/Fineart_Online/**) is a directory of about 1 200 Internet art resources. It is painting-oriented and points you to sites such as The First Impressionist Exhibit, 1874 (**lonestar.texas.net/~mharden/74nadar.htm**) where impressionist artists, given a cold shoulder by "traditionalists," assembled together to display their work to the public. Cezanne, Degas, Monet, Morisot, Pissaro, Renoir, and Sisley never looked back! And OAR is a jump station to many more interesting and informative sites.

The WebMuseum (**watt.emf.net/louvre**) has a fair collection of images of famous as well as lesser-known paintings. The traffic through this gateway is astounding—it has 200 000 visitors a week!

Performing Arts

Yahoo Canada (**www.yahoo.ca**) is again a good first stop for information on local stage and live theatre. Keep clicking through their "Arts" sub-directories until you're "local" enough to actually catch the show.

For even more stage and theatre information, try using City.Net (**www.city.net**), a city guide that was described in the travel section of this chapter. This popular site will guide you through happenings about town! The number of cities and towns it's including is growing by the month.

Music

With the advent of RealAudio, the number of music-related sites on the Web has exploded. But it's not just audio that these multimedia Web sites have to offer. Their offerings also include music history, trivia, and pictures.

Online Music and Audio References (**www.art.net/Links/musicref.html**) hyperlinks you to musical artist pages, online music resources, and related Internet resources. It's a good "one-window" stop for information about everything to do with music and audio.

The ClassicalNet Home Page (**www.classical.net/music**) has composer information, reviews, and links to related sites. The Picture Gallery of Classical Composers (**spight.physics. unlv.edu/picgalr2.html**) does what the title says—with over 1 000 online images organized by name, nationality, and era.

OperaGlass (**rick.stanford.edu/opera/main.html**) provides histories of performances, summaries of famous and not-so-famous "works," libretti, pictures, and discographies. Its comprehensiveness makes this a popular site with fans of the opera form.

Jazznet at **www.jazznet.com/~lmcohen** has reviews of and links to jazz sites on the Web. Thus, it's another example of a good "first stop" resource that can lead you to related sites.

Ragtime Home Page (**www.ragtimers.org/~ragtimers**) is one place where you can enjoy good multimedia clips of this musical genre. Joplin, Scott, and Lamb, the big-three "fathers of ragtime" are profiled at this site. But so are others, and the site's links will take you to these profiles.

The Christian Music Directory (**www.ccmusic.org/cmd**) has information on CDs, videos, and artists. It's a popular site in North America for all age groups.

Search tools also come in handy when it comes to music. Al Carroll from Halifax (**althepal@fox.nstn.ca**) shows us how!

As a 75-year-old retired engineer, I became involved with the Internet mainly because of my son, Jim, and my oldest daughter, Mary. My son, in fact, was an Internet expert and author.

It was a Christmas Eve tradition in the family to have one family member play the piano, and another sing "The Mistletoe Bow." Unfortunately, we lost the words and music. Someone suggested that I search the Internet for *this piece of information. At that time I was not far re-moved from a newbie, but my first stab using Excite (**www.excite.com**) came up with the right page. There, I found the words and the musical chords to accompany the song.*

Cinema

You're seventy. You loved silent pictures as a kid. You bemoan the lack of videos on "silents." Fear not! You, and others of all ages will find this next resource to be quite the site—or should I say "sight!"

With over 100 000 hits from over 70 countries in its first three months, the American Film Institute has produced a gem. This site (**www.afionline.org/cinema**) lets you watch silent pictures on the Web! You view these short motion pictures on your monitor through a small, 5 by 6 cm window (that looks like a miniature theatre, actually). All you need is to download VDOnet video software (through an AFI page link found at this site).

As for something a bit more current, would you like to get your grandchild a Disney product? There's no better place to get such information than Disney's Web site at **www.disney.com**. Here, you can find information about videos and related products. Blatantly commercial, this Disney site nonetheless offers wholesome videos.

Finally, if all you want is up-to-date information about movies, The Internet Movie Database(**us.imdb.com/welcome.html**) provides you with it. It covers approximately 50 000 movies with over 550 000 filmography entries. Expanding continuously, this site also provides a search engine and index to help you find almost anything related to films and film-making.

Literature

Most book selling on the Internet relates to giving you access to traditional print editions via the Internet. In other words, the book that you order over the Internet is sent to you by mail. A second book "selling" approach allows for online browsing and downloading of text—sometimes for free.

One player under the first approach is Amazon.com (**www.amazon.com**), the definitive Internet bookseller. It bills itself as "Earth's Biggest Bookstore" and claims to have access to 2.5 million titles. Amazon.com doesn't actually have a warehouse per se. (The 2.5 million books represent what it can order rather than what it actually holds.) Amazon.com does, however, have a distribution model that allows you to get discounts on books, which you can order through their site. And it doesn't just sell books—it also gives you information about books.

But be careful with Internet-based booksellers. Although the discounts may initially look good, once you add shipping and handling, the savings can be marginal at best. You also have to wait for delivery and will miss out on what many consider to be the pleasure of browsing through a bookstore. However, it's a great resource if you're isolated, immobile, or need to get that hard-to-find book.

Book Wire (**www.bookwire.com**) is a repository of book and publisher information, listing about 600 other Internet booksellers like Amazon.com. It's also a good stop if you want to browse book reviews or information on booksellers.

The Online Books Page (**www.cs.cmu.edu/books.html**) deals with the second type of book "sharing" approach (online browsing or downloading). It contains a searchable index of thousands of online books that can be read completely for free. But you have to be wary of browsing time—your Internet fees may go up unless you have unlimited access. You'll also need Adobe Acrobat Reader software (found at **www.adobe.com**) to be able to read on-line publications properly. The software is free and you can even increase the size of the type if poor eyesight is an issue.

Literary Resources on the Net (**www.english.upenn.edu/~jlynch/ Lit**) has links to Web sites focusing on English and American literature. You can search by genre, such as classical, renaissance, and twentieth century works.

Bartlett's Book of Quotations, the online version, at **www. colubia.edu/acis/bartleby/bartlett**) is searchable by keyword or author. This famous resource is a delight when you're looking for information on that "famous quote."

Also, consider newsgroups and mailing lists. They represent a great way to discuss and get information on arts and literature since you access a wide base of personal opinions. And opinions are what art is all about. Usenet newsgroups, for example, focus on discussion about many forms of art. They include the general categories of **alt.arts, rec.arts, rec.arts.misc, rec.arts.fine**, and **clari.living.arts**. Within these, there can be found countless sub-categories of interactive resources. And as for mailing lists, the Museum Discussion List can be subscribed to by sending the message "subscribe museum-L Your Name" to **listserv@unmvma.unm.edu**.

You Only Live Twice

As you enter the second half of your life, the issue of your mortality comes to the fore. For many persons at this stage of life, and perhaps for you, spiritual issues are examined more closely. Persons who are willing to examine their faiths are on a collision course with the many religious organizations that have recognized and acted on the fact that "getting the message out" is their *raison d'être*. More importantly, they have recognized that the Internet is a powerful way to reach others. And aside from organizations, many local churches are coming online, recognizing that they can reach many people this way.

Be warned, however, that the Net can also be dangerous in this area. Witness the emergence of cults and other dubious "religions" on the Net. Many such organizations are online for one purpose only—to get your money. Be mindful of these groups.

Because of the sensitivity of this issue, I have taken an objective and safe approach to presenting spiritual resources on the Net. First, I have presented only the traditional faiths: Christian, Judaic, and Islamic. Second, I have steered clear of denominations—it's not for me to say which is "best." Third, I have presented mostly "gateway" Web sites, where Internet resources are revealed, but you make the decision on which are best to visit. Fourth, I have presented Web sites in proportion to how the underlying faiths are represented in Canada. Lastly, I have selected the better sites— those with good multimedia and content.

RealAudio, streaming technology, graphics, and other state-of-the-art Internet applications are alive and well at many of these sites. They make the learning experience very effective.

The Bible Gateway (**www.gospelcom.net**) is the world's most popular Web site of its kind, "accessed monthly by millions." As a Christian gateway, you can access Web pages from more than 70 different Christian organizations and groups. It boasts a searchable online bible in multi-versions (including NIV, NASB, and others) and in seven languages. You can browse the site's extensive index by subject or service provided. You can search a famous biblical quote or browse their "Reasons to Believe" pages (**www.gospelcom. net/rbc/10rsn.home**). Its resources are often presented in RealAudio, making the learning experience easier.

If you have bible or faith-related questions, Christian Answers.Net (**www.christiananswers.net**) provides a database of almost 1 000 files addressing questions on creation versus evolution, theology, biblical archaeology, family, and social mores. It boasts 1 200 animation, graphic, and sound files. This site's question and answer format is its strongest feature and is what is driving its growth.

The Institute for Christian Leadership (**www.iclnet.org**) is a gateway to Christian online resources (utilizing Web, newsgroup, Gopher, etc.), literature, and even software. This comprehensive site is for those laypersons and scholars who want even more access to related information.

Judaism and Jewish Resources (**shamash.org/trb/judaism.html**) is a huge gateway to Jewish resources. The resources deal with the nation-state of Israel, Jewish studies and learning, and related worldwide networks and organizations. Online resources include Web, newsgroup, Gopher, and FTP content and applications. Pointers to books, archaeological findings, and news can also be found at this Web site.

For information on all major faiths, a good gateway is Finding God in Cyberspace (**users.ox.ac.uk/~mikef/durham/gresham. html**). The Internet resources are organized by person, print, digital, and teaching categories. Faiths linked to this site include Christianity, Judaism, Islam, and Hindu.

Breaking News

Traditionally, retired persons (and many over fifty) have always been big consumers of news. They often have more time to digest daily news and current events stories. Also, they have developed interests in very specific areas over the years, and possess an appetite for even more specialized information. Whether your current preferred news media are magazines, newspapers, radio news, current affairs TV broadcasts, or a combination of these, the Internet is a convenient alternative to these media. And the Net is equally responsive to anyone seeking even more specific information. This section will show you how.

The Times They Are A-Changin'

Most traditional publishers of newspapers and magazines—the printed news providers—now have a Web presence. Radio news is also making its way unto the Web. And programs such as Canada AM also can be accessed there. These providers have both conventional and Web-based services. So what's the difference between the old and the new? Basically, two big changes happened in the way that news could be accessed. The first is that with the Net, timing is less critical. In other words, if you missed a past newspaper issue, radio broadcast, or TV newscast, all is not lost because you can still access the archived news on the Net! The second, even more significant breakthrough in news accessibility is that not only can you retrieve very specific news from the Net, you can now "ask" the Net to get it for you, as it happens! This "push news" technology was presented in chapter 3.

While all this was happening, new "Internet companies" (delivering only online news) cropped up. They are vying to deliver electronic news to you; and they're locked head-to-head in a battle with the traditional news providers (online or not) for your "eyes and ears". The bottom line is that traditional mass media won't ever be replaced by the Web. There is simply no compelling reason to believe that anyone would actually prefer to be in front of a PC to get news at the expense of being on a porch with a radio or a newspaper in hand. Nevertheless, Net-based news will be a very effective, interesting, and convenient way to augment traditional news access.

Choices of News—before and after

Before the Net

News = Print + Radio + TV (Traditional Media)

After the Net

News = Print + Radio + TV
      and/or Online Versions of Traditional Media News
      and/or Internet News Companies (Text, Audio, Visual)

News through the Net

With the Internet, "traditional" news providers also allow you to browse their Web-based news content directly. CANOE (Canadian Online Explorer) at **www.canoe.ca,** is an example of how you can access traditional provider news on the Web. Another is the New York Times (**www.nytimes.com**). Both sites excel in their class and are considered to be in the vanguard of online news

Another way to get news (or other information) is through "push technology"—typically delivered by Internet companies. Unlike the process of accessing news by yourself ("pulling" in Web news or radio news into your PC), certain news providers (Internet companies) exist that "push" this news into your PC. This service can be utilized as either a "for free" or "for fee" arrangement— depending on the provider—and is gaining popularity with those whose time is limited. It's also being embraced by persons who have a real desire to access specific news but just don't know where to turn to on the Web.

Next, we will explore several of these Web-based news retrieval services. You will be introduced to the key providers of such information. The key thing to keep in mind here is that the focus is not on "what" information you get, but "how" you get it.

Traditional News Providers—Print, Radio, and TV on the Web

By now, you know that directories such as Yahoo can take you to the sites of news publishers such as the *Calgary Herald*, *Toronto Star*, or *Winnipeg Free Press*. They can also take you to *Macleans*, *Time Magazine* and even radio sites on the Web. If you already know their direct URL's (addresses), all the better.

Printed News on the Web

One-stop repositories of Web pages or links are always a good first call. Editor and Publisher Interactive (**www.mediainfo.com**) has about 1 200 media links organized by country. Canadian newspapers are organized by province. Newslink (**www.newslink.org**) is a similar site. And news and press releases can be accessed at **www.newswire.ca**. Newswire provides real-time information and is the largest database of its kind in Canada. Its 50 000 news releases from 75 countries can be searched by organization, industry, keyword, category, or subject.

As mentioned above, CANOE (**www.canoe.ca**) and the New York Times (**www.nytimes.com**) are good examples of online newspaper resources.

But do keep in mind that full online editions of these publications usually come with a fee—unless you're already a subscriber to their print editions. Essentially, if you have to pay for a printed newspaper, you'll also have to pay for its full online version. However, full text extracts of daily editions are plentiful and can, in fact, be accessed for free. Canoe is an example of such a resource.

Radio News on the Web

Radio has entered the Web! The Internet advantage with Web radio news is that you're not restricted to frequency bandwidth. In other words, you can "listen" online to a radio station in New Mexico!

If you enjoy CBC Radio and wish to see what it offers on the Web, browse the CBC Radio Web site at (**www.radio.cbc.ca**). Here, you can retrieve old broadcasts in RealAudio or text or you can browse through their archives to select a topic that interests you. CBS Radio Networks (**www.cbsradio.com**) has the *CBS News* and the popular *Osgood File*. It's good for accessing U.S. news. If you want to listen to something more cosmopolitan, try the MIT List of Radio Stations on the Net, a specialized directory of international radio stations at **wmbr.mit.edu/stations/list.html**. It has a searchable database of over 2 200 radio stations worldwide, including many Canadian ones.

What about something closer to home? Easy. Just enter the call letters of local radio stations (add the word "radio" to the call letters) into your browser. You may find one or two local radio Web sites this way.

AudioNet (**www.audionet.com**) has an extensive directory to audio sites such as those developed by radio stations and record companies. And Timecast (**www.timecast.com**) bills itself as the quintessential RealAudio guide. Here, there are links to audio sites—radio as well as TV Web pages.

Television on the Web

Yes, TV is also coming to the Net. Or should I say "the Net is coming to TV?" Actually, it's a bit of both. In 1997, software giant Microsoft signalled its confidence in cable-delivered Net services by buying the fourth-largest cable service provider in the U.S. Eventually, cable delivery of Internet content will grow at full speed. Now, it's still in its infancy. Most of Microsoft's actions are bellwethers of things to come in the world of technology. In this way, the Net is coming to TV.

In the meantime, TV stations are advertising their existence through the Web. These stations or networks may provide you with some or all of the following:

- Coming broadcast previews
- Past program transcripts
- Live audio feed
- Weather, sports, business, and current affairs information
- Video broadcasts

As for video, it takes a long time to download it from the Net to your PC, so don't be surprised that "TV on the Web," in its current form, usually includes everything but lots of video signals.

In terms of getting there, a good place to start is, of course, a directory. There's a specialized directory of worldwide TV stations that have a Web presence. Ultimate TV (**www.ultimatetv.com**) is that resource. *Canada AM* (**www.baton.com**), *Newsworld* (**www.newsworld.cbc.ca**), and other Canadian productions can be found there. From Ultimate TV, you can get access information about newscasts, shows, and TV channels and listings. Worldwide stories, and morning and evening news clips can also be accessed.

The pickings from U.S. TV stations are even more plentiful than those from Canadian stations

U.S. Television Stations on the Net	
DateLine NBC	**www.msnbc.com/Onair/nbc/dateline/default.asp**
48 Hours	**www.cbs.com/primetime/48_hours.html**
FOX News	**foxnews.com**
PBS	**www.pbs.org**
60 Minutes	**www.cbs.com/primetime/60_min.html**
The Weather Channel	**www.weather.com**

Combinations of Text, Audio, and Video

CNN Interactive (**www.cnn.com**) provides news on world events, financial topics, health, weather, travel, and lifestyle issues. They also let you search their archives for past news. Various forms of presentation are used. For example, RealAudio, video streaming, and real-time technology is either being applied now or will be applied soon at this site. CNN Interactive also provides current news coverage of sports, politics, and technology. CNNfn is another option at this site that allows you to track stocks, mutual funds, and other financial instruments on a real-time basis. You can download company stock information or click on a company's Web site and go directly to it!

Services very similar to those above are offered by Reuters NewMedia (**www.reuters.com**) and Trib.com News (**www.trib.com**).

For a good directory of "combination" online news resources, visit the Investigative Journalism on the Internet site (**www.vir.com/~sher/paperstv.htm**). There you can find referrals and links to print, radio, and TV Web sites. Another, more international version of this type of site is Media Online Yellow Pages (**www.webcom.com/~nlnnet/yellowp.html**).

Chapter 9

The Fifty-Plus Bill of Rights

Thus far in this book, I have revealed some of the many Internet resources that can be harnessed by persons over fifty to help them with key issues in areas such as finance, health, housing, and leisure. To be sure, these general issues are not the exclusive domain of retirees or near-retirees. This chapter, however, is dedicated to the discussion of those online resources specifically designed for retirees or near-retirees.

The people shaping the Net have recognized the importance of the need for "fifty-plus" information. But what exactly is this information? What is it that you care about most? As someone over fifty, do you not have the right to timely, relevant, accurate, and useful information?

Before the Internet became an option for accessing information, you had to haphazardly "look around" for important "fifty-plus" information. Now, the Internet empowers you to take full advantage of your right to this age-specific information. Exactly what is this "important" and "useful" information? It's what I refer to as your "Fifty-Plus Bill of Rights!" The table below presents the elements of these rights.

Fifty-Plus Bill of Rights

All mature Canadians have a right of access to information that is useful and important to them—persons over fifty. This information is provided by various groups and includes:

Associations	Products, services, lifestyle options, and advocacy geared to helping those over fifty.
Non-profit groups, clubs, and other organizations with an Internet presence	Services and activities for mature Canadians
Consumer protection and awareness groups	Consumer awareness for older Canadians
Legal assistance providers	Government and private legal services catering to the needs of those over fifty

If you possess a good awareness of your "Fifty-Plus Bill of Rights,"—the right to access "fifty-plus" information from relevant information providers—you will stand to save money, become a more active citizen, be alert to fraud, and have affordable access to legal protection. These were always your rights! The problem, however, was your ability to access this information—to execute these rights. This is because the gap between a right and ability to access a right, can sometimes be very wide. But with the Internet, a wealth of "fifty-plus" information is unlocked. Your right to information comes to fruition. In fact, it's incredible just how much "fifty-plus" online information there really is out there. And even though some Web sites to be presented here are U.S.-based, their content is generic enough so as to apply to all Canadians over fifty. These resources will set you off on your way to getting needed information.

This chapter will serve to tip the first domino. The effect to you will be one that is fascinating, informative, and empowering!

L.J. Klein (**ljklein1@ix.netcom.com**) (age 66 and CARP member) of Shepherdsville, Kentucky, aptly describes his vision of the rights and roles of seniors, and how the Internet has empowered seniors and changed society in general. His personal account embodies the spirit of seniors' advocacy.

> *The Internet is to the present and the future what newsprint was to the first 150 years of North America. It is what radio became to the next generations and what television became to the next and to our generation.*
>
> *Contrary to common concepts, seniors are overall more adept at utilizing the Internet and the technical aspects of active computing than most other major population groups. Furthermore, there are "senior-net" [such as Fifty-Plus.Net] applications (far superior to any "community" substitutes), chat areas, bulletin boards, and newsgroups. We, as a group, are mature, experienced, and tolerant—except in matters of sex, politics, and religion.*
>
> *One can and should use the Internet to keep abreast of the modern world, to keep ahead of our children, to be competent, to lead and educate our grandchildren and others who seek our advice. It's where we get the stimulus to grow intellectually, and remain interested in life. I think that the Net actually prolongs our lives and productivity. For most of us, the most facile pathways to all of this are by way of the senior-oriented online organizations both in Canada and in the United States.*

Speaking of advocacy and seniors services groups, let's look at some next.

Associations

The Canadian Association of Retired Persons (CARP)

There are many provincial and "special interest" associations that exist to serve the needs of retirees and near-retirees. However, there is only one national organization that speaks out for all Canadians and that also has a comprehensive Web site that you can access—CARP.

CARP is "a national, non-profit organization representing individuals over fifty, retired or not." CARP's goals are to:

Preserve and protect the rights of those over fifty through advocacy.
Provide access to useful "fifty-plus" information.
Negotiate group discounts on products and services available to members.

The 325 000-member CARP has stepped boldly into the information age. Through Fifty-Plus.Net (**www.fifty-plus.net**), the on-line home of CARP and *CARP News*, it has extended its reach and provision of benefits to Canadians over fifty. Because Fifty-Plus.Net is so significant (that is, it is Canadian, comprehensive, and relevant), it is discussed in a separate section.

CARP is not publicly funded; and this is critical. Why? Because its lack of reliance on government means that it has an independent voice of advocacy and can therefore "blow the whistle" on governments that do not take the interests of those over fifty into account. Can you picture a government-funded organization doing this without consequence?

Local Associations

In Canada, there are many "seniors" associations that cater to provincial and local seniors' interests. Most of these are still not on the Net. Of the few that are, their Web content is often limited since volunteers can put only so much time into Web site development. I believe that many of these groups will eventually "get wired" or expand their existing Web sites. This is because information gathering and communication is their *raison d'étre*. Because even these smaller "offline" organizations still provide services and printed information (often free), you can always call them by phone—but how do you find their number?

Recall that in Part I, I introduced a valuable people and organization access tool: Canada 411 (**www.canada411.sympatico. ca**). With the Web, you can get the number of local seniors' organizations, associations, or clubs even if you don't know the name of the city they are located in. Try doing that with directory assistance on the telephone! Not only will you incur a hefty charge, you'll also play hit and miss if you can't provide the operator with a city name! Similarly, there are many times when you will hear an advocacy group's name on the radio but won't know how to reach it. With this Web site, it's a lot easier to find the information you need than the old methods.

In those cases where you don't quite know the name but know it had "seniors" and "Manitoba" in it, try the search tools and directories. You'd be surprised how often they'll help you find the exact name.

Community Resources

Nothing beats a local Freenet to access community information. In many cases, there is a sub-directory for seniors' community events.

The Calgary Free-Net (**www.freenet.calgary.ab.ca/populati/ communit/Seniors/sen_menu.html**), a regional Internet resource, provides information that is of interest to not only Albertans but also all mature Canadians. This is because in addition to community events, many such sites contain generic information that is useful to all seniors. Many "fifty-plus" Web sites provide links to Freenets and similar local information.

Fifty-Plus.Net

Although other seniors' organizations may eventually get online, it would be difficult for them to catch up to Fifty-Plus.Net in comprehensiveness and quality-of-content. Not as long as Dan Goldhar is running it! I say with complete confidence and objectivity that Dan's tireless efforts in designing, building, updating, and promoting CARP's site will likely remain unmatched. But the real asset that he brings into Fifty-Plus.Net is his dedication to and understanding of your Fifty-Plus Bill of Rights—your right to important and helpful information!

Fifty-Plus.Net has lots of original content that deals with your right of access to:

1. Organizations providing you with discounted products and services,
2. Non-profit groups, clubs, and other organizations with an Internet presence,
3. Consumer protection and awareness groups,
4. Legal assistance providers, and
5. Government resources.

Notice the pattern? All of your Fifty-Plus Bill of Rights "bases" are covered. And the site is well organized with respect to key retirement management issues too—finances, health, housing, advocacy, and lifestyle.

Fifty-Plus.Net has information on membership, its publication

CARP News, learning resources, current events, leisure options, retirement home and community information, special deals, and more.

Dan Goldhar, (**gmanager@fifty-plus.net**), vice-president and general manager of Fifty-Plus.Net (also marketing representative at *CARP News*) is excited about the role that his Web site plays in protecting the interests of those Canadians who are over fifty years of age. It is clear from his TV talk show and radio broadcast efforts that he's a bona fide believer in the importance of conveying good information to everyone. Unlike other seniors' group Web sites, there is no overly-specialized mandate here. Fifty-Plus.Net hits the mark on all Canadian retirement management issues and allows you to execute your right to important "fifty-plus" information.

But how was Dan Goldhar's interest in the Net sparked? What was his personal Internet story? Here's what Dan has to say:

> *Things like the Internet have always fascinated me. Log and timber-frame homes were once a serious interest of mine because they were unique and represented a developing trend in alternative home building. If something is new and different, I have always taken an interest, but not always to the same extent or with the same results.*
>
> *Thanks to the support and encouragement of my wife, Janet, I was led into the world of computers and the Internet at the tender age of 38. As true a neophyte as there ever was, I was intimidated by computers and not convinced of the fact that they could add to my life.*
>
> *I enrolled in a course at a computer school and, along with 30 others, attempted to learn the basics. Three months later I graduated, only to discover that my newly-acquired skills needed to be upgraded almost the instant I walked out the door!*
>
> *But I was hooked; I purchased a used computer for $30*

and signed up with the only Internet service provider I could find. That was in January 1994.

My early-life online experience consisted of Internet Relay Chats (IRC) with other early adapters from many parts of the world including Australia, Singapore, and Israel. My e-mail reader was a text-based program called Pine.

Like all new users of that era, I struggled with many of the complicated codes that were part of the programming language and I bought books and learned. I was addicted and my wife soon began calling herself an Internet widow. In January 1996, with the support of Lillian Morgenthau, President of the Canadian Association of Retired Persons (CARP), and CARP News publisher David Tafler, I began the process of realizing my dream of building a World Wide Web site.

Today, in what seems like a lifetime later, I am the general manager of Fifty-Plus.Net, the online home of CARP and CARPNews. We launched "Fifty-Plus.Net" on October 1, 1996 with 80 pages—we now provide information on over 300 pages. Thousands of people from all over the world visit us weekly.

We are embarking on an exciting journey and I encourage all those who read this book to take up the challenge. The experience will revitalize you and change your view of the world. It sure changed mine.

Now, let's take a closer look at Fifty-Plus.Net's hotlinks at **www. fifty-plus.net.**

Fifty-Plus.Net Resources and Links

In addition to Fifty-Plus.Net's solid proprietary content, which we will review shortly, this site provides strong links to related resources. Two of the Web site's areas, the "Retirement Choices and Tourism in Canada" pages and the "50+ Net Resources" pages (both accessed by clicking corresponding home page menu

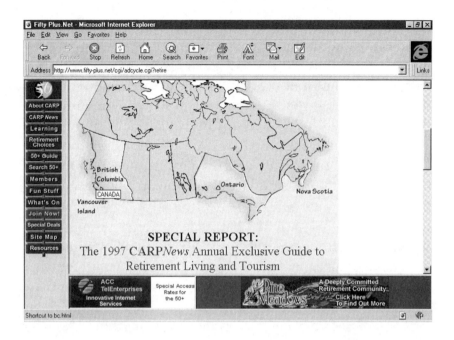

items) are especially interesting. The former is a perfect example of how easy-to-understand graphics are combined with useful content. Links are also provided to:

Investment information	Other CARP members and "fifty-plus" Web sites
Health issues	Volunteering options
Legal issues	Retirement management issues
Government resources	Publications

The Fifty-Plus.Net site is expanding every day as is evidenced by its aggressive "hit rate," publicly displayed on its home page.

Search 50+

With over 300 pages and counting, Fifty-Plus.Net has provided a search tool to navigate its site. But this is no ordinary search tool.

Aside from navigating its own Web site, this tool lets everyone, members or otherwise, access extracts of past issues of *CARP News*. If, for example, you're looking for information on registered retirement income funds (RRIFs), you can enter a keyword that will refer you to an extract of a previous *CARP News* article on the topic. It's very handy, and sure beats the "hit or miss" search approach. And speaking of RRIFs, David Tafler's *Everything You Ever Wanted to Know About RRIFs But Were Too Young to Ask* (ITP Nelson) can provide you with additional guidance.

50+ Net Guide
Whenever you're online and want to refresh your memory or learn more about an Internet tool (such as e-mail, Archie, etc.), but don't have a book handy, go to this "New User" guide area. Click on "50+ Net Guide" to access it. You'll be able to learn about some of the new Web applications that are planned for this site in the near future. And this reference resource will expand over time, along with the Net!

CARP
As mentioned before, advocacy (preserving and protecting "fifty-plus" rights) is a key mandate of CARP. To this end, you can find out what CARP is doing through their hotlink icon. There, you can access their online polls. One poll, whose results initially took me by surprise, reinforced the need for Internet-based (as well as published) information to seniors. This internal but statistically significant poll revealed that one third of respondents were not aware of the proposed but imminent Seniors Benefit Plan. This affects everyone over 65, and many younger people too!

CARP's governmental interactions are also outlined here; as are their press releases. If you're not up-to-date on these issues, you're missing out on a great chance to speak out through CARP. The membership fee is nominal and the benefits translate into helping yourself (through discounts) and others (through advocacy and politics). As you know, there is strength in numbers! If you want to add yours to those of other members, you can sign-up online or offline.

CARP News

CARP News represents publishing excellence. Why am I saying this? Actually, I'm not. Rather, the U.S.-based Mature Market Resource Centre is. In fact, CARP has won eleven of their awards for editorial excellence in a North American competition gauging the "best information produced for adults aged 50 and over."

Through Fifty-Plus.Net's site, members can access this literature online. Aside from being able to search the publication's database, you can access regular features such as "Destinations," the "Living With" health series, "Auto-Biography", and "Money Talk." As for Fifty-Plus.Net, there's a new daily article that can be easily accessed online.

The Learning Centre

This area of Fifty-Plus.Net refers you directly to sponsor sites. The material found here is not of a commercial nature. Rather, it is a repository of informative and educational material. The links here are expanding monthly.

Special Deals

You should keep in mind that another key mandate of CARP is to provide members and non-members alike with special pricing on various products and services. These include discounts on books, computers, and other goods and services. Discounts can also be obtained indirectly through other Fifty-Plus.Net Web pages, where sponsors offer seniors' packages and discounts. You can also get an online automobile insurance quote, which saves both time and paperwork.

What's On

At these event listing pages, a wealth of entertainment and recreational information is provided. Geared to events of interest to the "fifty-plus" group, this Web site area is likely to expand soon from its current Ontario and B.C. focus.

Lastly, remember that the Fifty-Plus.Net site is continually evolving. Although it boasts a highly respectable 20 000 transfers or "page flips" a week, CARP is planning to expand content even further. Also planned at the time this book went to print are chat lines, a "Job Mart" section, and a "cyberpal" feature.

More Fifty-Plus Organizations on the Net

When you're browsing through the Web, you'll come across many "fifty-plus" or related sites. But how do you know if they are good? What's their angle? As with any other issue (such as health or finances), you have to exercise caution when looking at any special interest Web site.

The table below provides a checklist of questions to ask yourself when browsing through "advocacy" or "special interest" Web pages. While most special interest sites are probably fine—as are all of the sites presented in this chapter—it only take one bad source of information to lead you to a bad decision or unduly influenced point of view.

Questions to Ask Yourself about Special Interest Web Sites

Is the organization sponsoring the Web site clearly identified?
Is the purpose and mandate of the organization clear?
Is an address and phone number given to help verify the legitimacy of the organization?

Is there a listing of sources to help verify facts and statistics presented?

Is the site professional-looking?

Is Web advertising clearly set apart from content?

Does Web content emphasize or favour advertisers more than the organization's own mandate (that is, is it biased)?

Are Web pages current?

Are opinions supported by facts, or at least common sense?

Now, armed with these caveats, let's look at some more "fifty-plus"-oriented Web sites, including international as well as Canadian resources.

Indices

A constant lesson emphasized throughout this book has been that a good starting point to a search for a Web site is an index. Selected Sites of Interest to Seniors (**www.mbnet.mb.ca/crm/other/genworld/sources2.html**) is a page that provides a huge index (about 100 links) to other seniors' sites. Many topics are covered and are organized under key retirement management themes (such as finances, health, housing, and lifestyle). A related set of pages can also be accessed at (**www.mbnet.mb.ca/crm/other/genworld/sources.html**), where "fifty-plus" resources are organized by type of information resource rather than by topic. For example, you can access popular newsgroups, Freenets, FTP sites, chat lines, E-zines, and Web pages. You can also use their time-saving links to other seniors' sites. By the way, these pages belong to the Seniors' Computer Information Project (**www.mbnet.mb.ca/crm**), a well-organized Canadian site of interest to all seniors.

You'll have to get your mouse oiled for this next site—it's got over 5 500 U.S. and Canadian Web pages accessed through various links. Age of Reason (**www.ageofreason.com**) is a practical and comprehensive resource for mature individuals that provides topical coverage in the areas of employment (post your résumé to a job bank), housing (explore your options), shopping (get special seniors' discounts), veteran's affairs, pensions, travel (browse the cruise, flight, hotel, and provincial tourism page links), literature (read or publish your own verse) and hobbies (research gardening and collecting). It is a well-used site, judging by the Web site hits it reports.

The Seniors Site (**seniors-site.com**) is a very comprehensive, quasi-index type of resource. Its pages and links are organized according to basic retirement management themes. Although U.S.-focussed, much of its content (such as that pertaining to health-care) is nonetheless relevant to Canadians. Information to caregivers is also a key focus of this site.

Eldercare-Oriented Sites

The term "eldercare" refers to elderly people who have healthcare or other care needs. It's not just a health issue—it's also a mobility and natural ageing issue. The National Aging Information Center states that 7 million people in North America that are 65 or older and who are non-institutionalized have either mobility or self-care limitations.

Many persons over fifty are still responsible for the care of frail family elders. As life expectancies increase, and as resources (for example long-tern care beds) become more scarce, the care of elders is an issue that grows in importance every day. There is a very real need to know what other persons facing this important issue are doing. There is a need for information about health care, housing, and end-of-life matters.

Unfortunately, many caregivers may not reside in the same city as their charges. They lack access to information on available programs and services. With the Web, they can now access this eldercare information.

Eldercare Web (**www.ice.net/~kstevens**) is a source of such information. The information found here is not just about long-term health-care—it's also about related issues such as grief, respite care, and caregiver obstacles. Also, you can access aging, quality of life, social, research-oriented, and financial information at this site. Eldercare Web is equally valuable for caregivers themselves, many of whom are over fifty.

Another good eldercare-oriented site is Senior Link (**www. seniorlink.com**). This eldercare resource lets you access information on home safety, medical conditions, nursing homes, mental health resources, and general retirement planning. Although it's U.S. based, much of its information is generic enough to be useful to you. This site will appeal to both seniors and caregivers alike.

50+ Only

One site where you have nothing to worry about in terms of legitimacy is CARP's sister organization, the American Association of Retired Persons (AARP) at (**www.aarp.org**). Like Fifty-Plus.Net, AARP's own online voice and Web site also contains a broad index of useful information, interactivity, and links to other sites. This colossal association has over 35 million members over 50 years of age. It provides "fifty-plus" information about finances, insurance, health, housing, advocacy, travel, and leisure issues. A visit to this site is always worthwhile, even if you are Canadian.

SeniorNet (**seniornet.org**) is an international organization of 25 000 seniors whose mission is to promote the Internet through teaching, information-sharing, and other means. Online resources include a book club, their SeniorNet Cafe, an introduction forum, and a discussion group. Like CARP, they are pioneers in using the Internet as a tool to serve the needs of those over fifty.

Seniors on the Web (**www.southam.com/edmontonjournal/sens/**

sensindex.html) offers two simple services. The first is a reasonable set of links to "fifty-plus" and related sites. But its most interesting service is that it compiles and summarizes the current weeks' "seniors" news stories. The fact that it reports stories is not at all surprising—this is a Southam newspaper Web site!

Senior.Com (**www.senior.com**) is a comprehensive referral resource to online and other information. Topics include finance, leisure, and shopping. In addition, it allows you access to its chat area (**www.Senior.com/chat/**) where you can select one of several "chat rooms": The 50+ Lounge, The Singles Room, Events, and Caregiver Support.

The National Aging Information Center's site (**www.ageinfo.org**) is a U.S. resource that has a searchable database of information geared to all persons over fifty. It's also an excellent source for referrals to other information sources. Much of this demographic, social, health, and economic information also applies to Canadians over fifty.

Today's Seniors (**novatech.on.ca/seniors**), the online version of the Canadian seniors' publication, lets you access editorials, features from past issues, entertainment events, lifestyle, and leisure information. You can access travel resources that are organized by both destination and mode of travel. It also deals with retirement management themes such as finance, health, and housing by allowing you access to archived articles of previous issues.

Seniors' Home Pages (**www.mbnet.mb.ca/crm/seniorhp.html**) is a collection of home pages of mature North Americans. It also has good links to seniors-only sites.

Fifty Plus R Us (**shrinvest.com/shr.html**), an online, advocacy-related soapbox to stand on, lets you vent some of your more "controversial" opinions.

Senior Lifestyle Magazine (www.senior-lifestyle.com) launched an Internet version of its popular California-based publication. It deals with leisure and the active senior. Thus, it applies to everyone—regardless of residency.

Genealogy Resources

If you're trying to find a missing link in your family tree, the Net can provide you with a road map to find it. Although genealogy is of interest to all age groups, persons over fifty have claimed it as their own. After all, they're in an ideal position to add to their existing family tree. Genealogy is not so much a leisure activity as it is a research exercise. Mature persons the world over love genealogy. How do I know?

The Genealogy Home Page (GHP) at **www.genhomepage.com** boasted well over half a million visits since its inception date in late 1996. Predominantly a U.S. Web site, GHP nonetheless has extensive resources for Canadians as well as people outside of North America. At this site, you can access archives, deeds, maps, and other tools of the genealogical trade. Also, related newsgroups and mailing lists are listed here. Many useful links are provided—a key ingredient of a good genealogy Web resource. Finally, listings of North American societies are provided should you wish to find out more about them.

A distinctly Canadian genealogy resource is the Canadian Genealogy and History site (**www.islandnet.com/~jveinot/cghl/cghl.html**). It provides you with useful provincial resources—census data, provincial and national archives (church, marriage, death, and deeds), and referrals to local genealogical organizations. At this site, you can create a family tree by drawing on the site's database of historical information and statistical overviews. Like GHP, it's a "how to" genealogical resource more than a "detective" one (that finds the person for you); but it's complete.

Other genealogical resources to consider include newsgroups such as **alt.genealogy** and **soc.genealogy.misc.**

Other Missing Links

You may want to access a mailing list or discussion group that deals with "special interests" such as "seniors" or "retirement." You may also want to talk online with other people through newsgroups. It so happens that seniors' advocacy issues are inherently suited to mailing list, discussion group, and newsgroup formats. How do you find these ever-changing special interest or seniors' mailing lists, discussion groups, and newsgroups? By using the following three indices:

- Vivian Neou's List of Lists (**catalog.com/vivian/ interest-group-search.html**)
- Tile.Net/Lists (**tile.net/lists**)
- The Liszt Directory (**www.liszt.com**)

The process of using these particular resources—their nuts and bolts—was discussed in Part I.

Consumer Protection and Advocacy Groups

Consumer advocacy is not just about passively monitoring your rights. It's about pro-active deal-making and bargain-hunting (the good), staying away from poor purchases (the bad), and aggressively reporting scams (the ugly).

Drawing Near to the Good

As we have already seen, Fifty-Plus.Net (**www.fifty-plus.net**) provides Canadian members of CARP, and even visitors, with many product and service discounts. Mature Canadian Web sites such as Fifty-Plus.Net often stake their name on the quality of discounted products and services appearing in their online or printed publications. The lesson? Seek out products and services that appear (that are "referred to" or otherwise found) on the Web sites of credible, well-known organizations such as CARP.

There is another useful consumer advocacy-oriented Web site that you should know about. It's one of those commercial "one-stop," index-type sites that makes Web searches for reviewed commercial products and services easier. While the Consumer World (**www.consumerworld.org**) site is not geared exclusively to mature Canadians, it is noteworthy, having gathered about 1 500 of "the most useful consumer resources on the Net." The following site is an example of a resource I found by following one of Consumer World's links.

If you're buying a car (one of life's larger purchases) you need good information about accessories and price. Consumer World has a link to one of the most popular Internet sites dealing with

cars—the Edmunds Web site. (You can also go there directly (**www.edmunds.com**)). At this site, you can obtain dealer invoice and suggested retail prices, online safety reports and "Buyer Advice" publications, new and used car ratings, and new car road test and preview information. Since automotive purchases represent big ticket items, the information at the Edmunds car site can potentially save you money "down the road."

Staying Away from the Bad

The anonymity of Internet salespersons makes it hard to find them. This is especially true if they're slippery fraud artists. Persons over fifty are regular targets of fraud. A visit to the U.S. National Fraud Information Center (**www.fraud.org/specinfo.htm**) seniors' page will tell you why. This page has advice and tips on how to avoid Internet, telephone, shopping, and other forms of fraud.

If you believe that you or one of your friends has been victimized in any of these ways, advice is provided on how you can confirm your suspicions and how you can help yourself or your friend.

Remember that if anyone tells you that you won a prize but you have to pay the "taxes" up front, hang up!

Reporting the Ugly

If you fell prey to the bad and want to report the ugly, what do you do next? You've heard of the Better Business Bureau (BBB), but maybe you don't exactly know what they can do to help you. Maybe you're not even sure where yours is located.

The Canadian BBB (**www.bbb.org/bureaus/canadian.html**) can help you locate the BBB office closest to you. The BBB Web pages are also well-stocked with useful online information including helpful online and printed publications, recent news and alerts, and other resources. Their advice includes how to resolve disputes with companies and how to make sure a charity is legitimate.

Legal Assistance on the Net

Canadians over fifty are at a stage in life when major financial, housing, and lifestyle choices come to the fore. Typical examples of these issues include estate planning, moving to a new home, and moving abroad. In such cases, you'll likely be turning to a lawyer for help. And with the Internet, you can be better prepared to deal with a lawyer, whether she's your existing one or a new prospect.

Online legal assistance takes on various forms. Legal assistance or information can be obtained through online government legal-aid programs, printed legal resources referred to online, and Web links to lawyers' practices. Some lawyers even provide online e-mail advice.

Provincial Legal Resources

The Law Society of Upper Canada (LSUC) at **www.lsuc.on.ca/ public_home.html,** one of several provincial Societies in Canada, provides basic legal advice and tips on the Internet.

By clicking on "Finding a Lawyer," you'll be presented with tips and advice on how to secure legal counsel, what to do when meeting your lawyer, how to maximize a lawyer's time, and how to keep costs down. You'll also be provided with a good overall checklist of questions to ask.

The LSUC's Public Legal Information Page (above) also allows you to obtain specific advice on employment, family, real estate, and criminal law. You can listen to advice (Top Ten Legal Topics) in Real Audio too, which you can download from this site. If you prefer, you can read the text only. It's totally up to you.

Clicking on the "Lawyers and Legal Assistance" icon at this site gives you access to more information on topics such as provincial

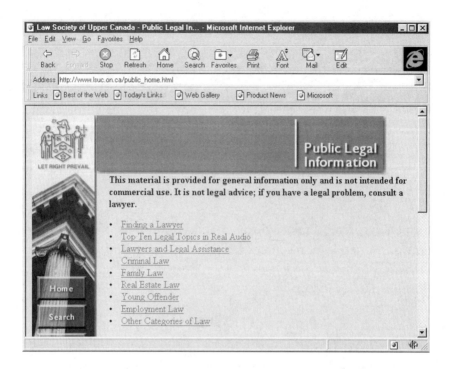

legal aid, disputing a legal bill, local community legal clinics, and para-legals. The information in the LSUC Web pages is generic enough for all Canadians and typifies what other provincial sites contain in their own Web pages. Where are these other provincial Web pages?

The Federation of Law Societies of Canada (**www.flsc.ca**), provides you with a directory of all provincial Law Societies in Canada. Here, you will get information more specific to your province—an important consideration given that legal information changes from jurisdiction to jurisdiction. Most provincial societies have links to lawyers practising in your province or territory.

Printed Legal Material and Directories

Carswell, a publisher of legal books and materials, has online information that may be of interest to you if you want to dig deeper into a particular legal issue. Click on their publications icon (**www.carswell.com**) to view a complete index. In addition, Carswell has an online directory of lawyers. What sets this one apart from most of the provincial sites is that by clicking on a map of Canada, you can locate your existing lawyer's or a new lawyer's e-mail address. If the lawyer has a Web site too, you can click its icon to go there. Why would you do this? To get online, direct advice.

Online Advice

Many lawyers, like other professionals, have been quick to advertise their services on the Net. The benefit to them is that they get broadened exposure. The benefit to you is that the better sites will allow you to get some good, free information in return. You may even choose to use that lawyer or just use the site to do some price comparisons.

Personal online queries to a lawyer are typically initiated by e-mail. Your initial queries would be along the lines of the online list of questions provided at the LSUC site (see the "Finding a Lawyer" page discussed there). The Carswell site above has a good directory for this type of search.

Caveat Emptor!

One last word about legal-oriented Web sites. Most of these sites are accessible free of charge and contain highly relevant and useful information. However, almost all lawyer Web sites also advertise services that are intended to be rendered to you for a fee. Know how to distinguish between the two motives. Know when to use a legal service. And when browsing the Web, it's very easy to forget where the information is coming from. Again, the geographic origin of legal information is very significant. Many legal sites will include a cautionary note reminding you that a law in one province may not apply in another. In case they don't, be mindful of this fact!

Appendix I

Additional Internet Sites

NOTE: All addresses of Internet resources presented in this appendix are preceded by "http://" (unless otherwise indicated). For example, the CANOE site below should be entered into your browser as: **http://www.canoe.ca/Money/home.html**. Also, the resources listed in this appendix are *in addition to* those already presented in the chapters.

Financial Management on the Web

Bank of Canada **www.bank-banque-canada.ca** Information on publications, market rates, CSBs, and monetary policy. Also, links to related sites.

CANOE **www.canoe.ca/Money/home.html** Up-to-date interest rates for GIC's, term deposits, and loans.

Etrade **www.canada.etrade.com** Internet online trading.

Fund Library **www.fundlib.com** Comprehensive mutual fund information on a site sponsored by over 20 fund companies.

InvestAlert **www.investalert.com** Unbiased mutual fund information.

IPO Data **www.ipodata.com** Initial public offering information.

IRS **www.irs.ustreas.gov/prod** Information on tax issues you will face if you move to the United states upon retirement.

The Syndicate **www.moneypages.com/syndicate** Directory of over 1 000 finance and stock market-related sites.

Back to Work and down to Business

Employment

Career Magazine   **www.careermag.com** Like MBNS (below), allows for an even more detailed keyword search of newsgroups by location, skills, and job type.

Classified Jobs in the SUN Media Corp.'s   **canoe1.canoe.ca/ Classified/JOBsearch.html** A good resource for locating many types of job listings.

Electronic Labor Exchange   **ele.ingenia.com** Free government-sponsored Web job-matching service.

IntelliMatch   **www.intellimatch.com** Service geared to businesspersons and those in high-technology matches résumés to employers.

JobNet   **www.westga.edu/~coop** A collection of newsgroup job postings from the Internet.

JobCenter   **www.jobcenter.com** Provides résumé and keyword-search services for a fee.

Job Match   **www.jcitech.com/jobmatch** An online job-matching service.

Kelly Services   **www.kellyservices.com** Information on placement services for temporary administrative, technical, and clerical positions.

Worknet   **www.entrenet.com/easi** Comprehensive list of Canadian prospective employees on the Net.

Newsgroups   **misc.jobs, misc.jobs.offered, misc.jobs.resumes, alt.jobs, biz.jobs.offered, comp.jobs, can.jobs, bc.jobs, ont.jobs, tor.jobs, sudbury.jobs** Never to be underestimated, newsgroups are great for getting job-related tips and referrals.

Entrepreneurship

AT&T Home Business Resources   **www.att.com/hbr**
Comprehensive, business-related issues can be accessed here.

BizWomen   **www.bizwomen.com** Networking and support network for women entrepreneurs and executives.

DISCscribe Home Business Resource Centre   **www.discribe.ca/ yourhbiz** Home business-related advice and online discussion.

Mauldin Inc. Business Planning Primer   **www.cam.org/~jmauld** Online business planning primer.

Health-Care on the Net

Cool Disability Resources on the Internet   **disability.com** Jump station to many resources devoted to disability issues.

Eyeville   **www.eyeville.com** Comprehensive collection and discussion of vision-related issues.

Foot and Ankle Index   **www.footandankle.com** Solutions to foot problems.

INDIE   **indie.ca** Repository of Internet resources related to disabilities.

Johns Hopkins Infonet: Patient Advocacy Groups   **infonet.welch. jhu.edu/advocacy.html** Comprehensive hot-list complied by the Johns Hopkins Medical Institutions Information Network for many medical ailments and conditions.

Mayo Clinic's O@sis   **www.mayo.ivi.com** the content on this site is growing steadily towards online encyclopaedia status.

PharmInfoNet   **pharminfo.com** Drug database and disease information source.

Prostate Cancer InfoLink   **www.comed.com/Prostate** Another referral source for information about prostate cancer.

Resources for Disabled Index   **www.aip.org/aip/urls/disable.html** Information repository for the disabled.

Sleep Medicine   **www.cloud9.net/~thorpy** Lists different types of sleep problems and refers readers to discussion groups and mailing lists.

The Dental Site   **www.dentalsite.com** General dental information.

U.S. National Library of Medicine   **www.nlm.nih.gov** Comprehensive database, list of publications, and links.

Women's Health Hot Line   **www.soft-design.com/softinfo/womens-health.html**   Online publication of womens' health-care issues.

Newsgroups   **clari.news.drugs, alt.support.eating-disord, alt.support.headaches.migraine, tnn.living.health, fj.life.health, alt.support.arthritis, misc.health.arthritis, alt.education.disabled, alt.support.anxiety-panic, alt.support.abuse-partners, alt.support.asthma, alt.support.diet, alt.support.stop-smoking, alt.support.divorce, alt.support.menopause**

Mailing ListLongevity

To: **listserv@vm.ege.edu.tr**   Message: subscribe Longevit Yourname

For those who want to discuss improvement in their quality of life.

Corel's Medical Series   **www.corel.com/products/medicalseries**   Web page leads you to more information about Corel's Medical Series collection of CD ROMs. The site is a relevant and content-rich resource as to titles and prices. Written for professionals and the public alike. Corel has upcoming titles on Cancer, Alzheimer's, Asthma, Diabetes, Sleep Disorders, and First Aid.

House and Home

Canadian Home Builders Association   **www.chba.ca**   For those who absolutely *must* have a new home.

Coldwell Banker   **www.coldwellbanker.com/**   Typical real estate company site which also provides a primer on the process of making an offer and a description of the terms you will likely encounter.

Crown Woldwide Movers   **www.crownww.com**   Worldwide move specialist.

Homelife   **www.homelife.com**   Another real estate company site.

Senior Links   **www.retirenet.com**   Comprehensive, worldwide information about retirement communities, vacation and rental properties, and related resources.

Leisure and Lifestyle

Travel

Attractions Canada **attractions.infocan.gc.ca** A comprehensive information centre with links to provincial parks, seasonal attraction listings, and weather statistics by province.

CheckIn—The Tourism Database **www.checkin.com/database. html** International tourism information.

Go Explore **go-explore.com** Travel destination profiles.

Preview Vacations Online **www.vacations.com** Selected travel destination information resource.

State of Arizona Home Page **www.state.az.us** Arizona information source.

Travel Map Information Page **www.cdc.gov/travel/travelmap.html** Up-to-date warnings of infectious diseases accessed through an on-screen world map when you click on your travel destination.

USA CityLink **usacitylink.com** An online listing of Web pages that feature U.S. states and cities.

Worldspan **www.worldspan.com** Worldwide travel destination information.

Newsgroups **rec.travel.**
Try these extensions: **air, asia, australia+nz, caribbean, cruises, europe, misc, usa-canada.**

Mailing Lists: Travel Advisories
To: **travel-advisories-request@stolaf.edu** Message:subscribe

Womens' Issues

Women's Connection Online **www.womenconnect.com**
Networking and womens' issues information.

Newsgroups **soc.women, soc.penpals**

Veterans' Issues

Newsgroup **soc.veterans**

Mailing List WWII

To: **listserv@ubvm.cc.buffalo.edu** Message: subscribe WWII-L Yourname. Discusses World War II tactics, strategies, politics, and more.

Shopping

Internet Shopping Network **www.internet.net** Large Internet mall offering computer products from about 1 000 companies.

Hobbies

Newsgroups

alt.radio.scanner.uk, rec.antiques, rec.collecting.coins, rec.collecting.stamps, rec.puzzles, rec.gardens, rec.gardens.roses, triangle.gardens, rec.railroad, rec.models. railroad, rec.crafts, rec.food, fj.rec.food, alt.food.coffee, alt.food.fat-free, alt.food.ice-cream, tnn.foods, tnn.foods. recipes

Sports and Recreation

Newsgroups

alt.sport.croquet, alt.sport.darts, alt.sports.basketball, alt.sports.baseball, alt.sports.college, alt.sports.football, alt.sports.hockey, alt.sports.soccer.european, rec.running, rec.sport, rec.birds, rec.crafts, rec.folk-dancing, rec.pets

Arts and Literature

Emergency Emergency   **www.catt.citri.edu.au/emergency**   Disaster-related stories, images, events, as well as safety information and references.

Encyclopedia Britannica Online   **www.eb.com**   Authoritative references, Britannica's latest article database, articles not yet printed by Britannica, Merriam-Webster's *Collegiate Dictionary*, and more.

Internet Movie Database FAQ   **us.imdb.com**   Comprehensive database providing up-to-date information on over 45 000 films.

Mailing List: Biblio

To: **biblio-request@iris.claremont.edu** Message: biblio
List discussing various aspects of fine book collecting (rare, first edition fine press, others). To subscribe, send a message to the indicated e-mail address with the text "biblio".

Newsgroups

rec.arts.misc, clari.living.arts, rec.arts.fine, clari.apbl.music, rec.arts.books

History

Holocaust   **soc.culture.jewish.holocaust**

News

ClariNet   **www.clarinet.com**   General news service distributing about 2 500 stories daily, segregated into more than 600 topical categories. Its sources include the very best in news sources. If your ISP subscribes to this service, this news service is yours for free.

Dow Jones Business Information Services   **bis.dowjones.com** Fee-based, custom, business-news clipping service encompassing over 1 750 worldwide business publications, newspapers, and newsletters.

Ensemble Information Systems   **www.ensemble.com** Provider of custom business news.

Farcast   **www.farcast.com** Fee-based service delivering news, sports, weather, and stock quotes to your e-mail address.

Pathfinder   **www.pathfinder.com** Online news and entertainment stories and electronic editions of Time Warner's popular magazines (such as *Time*, *People*, and *Life*).

The Electronic Telegraph   **www.telegraph.co.uk** Fast-loading, online newspaper.

USA Today   **www.usatoday.com** Top U.S. news stories and a thorough synopsis of the daily news in six categories: news, sports, money, life, weather, and computers.

Newsgroups   **clari.world.asia.hong_kong, clari.world.asia.india, clari.world.asia.japan, clari.world.europe.central, clari.world. europe.eastern, clari.world.europe.russia, clari.world.europe.uk, clari.world.mideast, clari.world.oceania.new_zealand**

You Only Live Twice

Newsgroups   **pdaxs.religion.christian, pdaxs.religion.jewish**

The Fifty-Plus Bill of Rights

Third Age   **www.thirdage.com** Web-based community for persons over fifty.

Market Place   **www.tv.cbc.ca/market** Comprehensive Canadian consumer resource.

Index